BEFORE

the Special Education

REFERRAL

BEFORE
the Special Education REFERRAL

Leading
Intervention
Teams

Matthew
Jennings

CORWIN
PRESS
A SAGE Company

For information:

Corwin Press
A SAGE Company
2455 Teller Road
Thousand Oaks, California 91320
www.corwinpress.com

SAGE India Pvt. Ltd.
B 1/I 1 Mohan Cooperative
Industrial Area
Mathura Road, New Delhi 110 044
India

SAGE Ltd.
1 Oliver's Yard
55 City Road
London EC1Y 1SP
United Kingdom

SAGE Asia-Pacific Pte. Ltd.
33 Pekin Street #02–01
Far East Square
Singapore 048763

Printed in the United States of America.

Library of Congress Cataloging-in-Publication Data

Jennings, Matthew.
 Before the special education referral : leading intervention teams/Matthew Jennings.
   p. cm.
 Includes bibliographical references and index.
 ISBN 978-1-4129-6690-0 (cloth)
 ISBN 978-1-4129-6691-7 (pbk.)
 1. Children with disabilities—Education—United States—Evaluation.
 2. Learning disabilities—Diagnosis—United States. 3. Disability evaluation—
United States. 4. Group work in education—United States. I. Title.

LC4031.J46 2009
371.9—dc22   2008026649

This book is printed on acid-free paper.

08   09   10   11   12   10   9   8   7   6   5   4   3   2   1

Acquisitions Editor:	Debra Stollenwerk
Editorial Assistant:	Allison Scott
Production Editor:	Jane Haenel
Copy Editor:	Sarah J. Duffy
Typesetter:	C&M Digitals (P) Ltd.
Proofreader:	Ellen Brink
Indexer:	Wendy Allex
Cover and Graphics Designer:	Lisa Riley

Contents

Preface

I have served in the roles of a prereferral intervention team member, team coordinator, and administrator responsible for a school district's prereferral intervention process. It has been my experience that these teams are ineffective, inefficient, and sometimes used in harmful ways.

At best, the prereferral intervention team process was viewed as a bureaucratic necessity to be tolerated. Staff members went through the motions of the process because it was required by the policies of their school district. At worst, the process was a mechanism used to prevent children from being evaluated for services they may have required. All students were required to be referred to the school's prereferral intervention team before the teacher could initiate an evaluation for special education services. As a result, services to students who obviously required them were delayed and those students fell further behind.

Not wanting to rely solely on my own experience, I have engaged in conversations about this process with countless teachers and school administrators. To my dismay, my experience is not unique. Teachers bring students who demonstrate the greatest academic, behavioral, and health challenges to a group that is both poorly designed and managed. As a result, teachers do not develop new strategies for assisting these students, teachers end up frustrated, and the students' situations do not improve.

Being dissatisfied with the status quo, I embarked on a journey to determine what the research literature on this topic could offer. Interestingly, I found a significant discrepancy between what was being advocated in the literature and what was being applied in schools. Though interesting, this is not surprising; the studies were not synthesized into a set of practical steps that school administrators could follow to design, manage, and lead their schools' prereferral intervention team process.

THE PURPOSE OF THIS BOOK

The content of this book is based on an extensive review of research literature on the topics of prereferral intervention teams, group dynamics, and team development. The review and analysis of this literature was a critical first step, but it was not the primary goal. Rather, my primary anticipated outcome is for readers to develop their ability to understand and apply a sequence of practical steps that, done correctly, will result in improvement of the quality of prereferral intervention programs.

A second anticipated outcome is for readers to develop their ability to understand and then strengthen the connection between prereferral intervention and response to intervention programs. Response to intervention is a concept currently receiving a great deal of attention among educators. In response to this attention, many schools and districts are creating new programs and structures designed to implement response-to-intervention models. This is usually unnecessary and sometimes counterproductive. Readers will see why the better alternative to meeting the intent of response to intervention may be the improvement and extension of existing prereferral intervention programs.

INTENDED AUDIENCE

The primary audiences for this book are the school and district staff members charged with implementing, managing, and leading prereferral intervention teams. Typically, this group includes principals, assistant principals, and supervisors or directors of special education, but it may also include guidance counselors or supervisors, basic skills staff, and Title I program coordinators.

Although not the primary audience, there are important reasons for upper-level district administrators to read this book as well. It has been my experience that their support and understanding is essential for successfully achieving the goals of change efforts that are focused on improving the quality of prereferral intervention programs. By familiarizing themselves with the content in this book, superintendents and assistant superintendents will gain the knowledge necessary for supporting those on the front lines of these improvement initiatives.

APPROACH

In Chapter 1, I introduce the reader prereferral intervention teams and the fictional character Ellen Santiago. In the following four chapters, the reader moves back and forth between Ellen's story and a description of research and practice.

Throughout the narrative, I help the reader understand the struggles and triumphs of an administrator seeking to improve the quality of her school's prereferral intervention program. Furthermore, Ellen's story provides a real-world context to better understand the application of the research and practices described.

In Chapter 6, I describe the methods for evaluating prereferral intervention activities. Chapter 7 focuses on connecting and strengthening the linkage between current prereferral intervention programs and response to intervention.

SPECIAL FEATURES

In writing this book, a major goal was to provide the reader with all of the tools necessary for implementing the model described. As a result, Resource A provides a step-by-step one-year plan that the reader can follow to successfully implement the activities described throughout this book. This synthesis makes it possible and practical to move from theory to action.

Resource B includes every reproducible form necessary for implementing and evaluating the prereferral intervention program described. Examples of completed versions of many of these forms are provided throughout the chapters.

Resource B also contains sample overhead transparencies that can be used for training staff members. A script that can be followed or modified to explain the content of these transparencies is found where each is introduced in the text. Similarly, training activities are introduced in the body of the text. Complete descriptions of these activities can be found in Resource B.

Finally, embedded in the chapters are tables and charts designed to increase the reader's understanding of the material. The tables provide quick summaries of the most critical points presented in the corresponding section of the text, and the charts give the reader the opportunity to visually follow the processes being described.

Acknowledgments

Corwin Press gratefully acknowledges the contributions of the following reviewers:

Jodie L. Greene
Coordinator of Special Education
Plumsted Township School District
New Egypt, New Jersey

Susan B. Strauss
Principal
Walter Panas High School
Cortlandt Manor, New York

Marian White-Hood
Director of Academics and Principal Support
See Forever Foundation and Maya Angelou Public Charter Schools
Washington, DC

Eleanor Love
Principal
Los Cerritos Middle School
Thousand Oaks, California

Maria Kaylor
Assistant Professor
The University of Texas at San Antonio
San Antonio, Texas

Debi Gartland
Professor of Special Education
Towson University
Towson, Maryland

About the Author

Matthew Jennings is currently the superintendent of schools for the Alexandria Township Public School System, in New Jersey. Prior to serving in this position, Dr. Jennings served as an assistant superintendent of schools, a director of student services, a supervisor of curriculum and instruction, and a classroom teacher. He earned his master's degree and doctorate in educational administration from Rutgers University.

In addition to presenting at numerous state and national conferences, Dr. Jennings has served as an organizational behavior consultant to school districts throughout New Jersey. He works as an adjunct professor for Rutgers University, where he teaches courses on curriculum development, school administration, and the supervision of instruction. His work has been published in *Kappan*, *Preventing School Failure*, *The New Jersey English Journal*, *Channels*, and *The Writing Teacher*. His most recent publication, *Leading Effective Meetings, Teams, and Work Groups in Districts and Schools*, was released by the Association for Supervision and Curriculum Development in June 2007.

When he is not spending time with his wife, MaryAnn, his children, Ryan and Tara, and their dog, Amber, Dr. Jennings enjoys time at the beach, competing in triathlons, and watching Rutgers football games.

CHAPTER ONE

An Introduction to Prereferral Intervention Teams

If there is dissatisfaction with the status quo, good. If there is ferment, so much the better. If there is restlessness, I am pleased. Then let there be ideas, and hard thought, and hard work.

—Hubert H. Humphrey

At this point in the new teacher orientation program, Mrs. Thompson felt agitated by her confusion. This was not because she was a new teacher. She had been teaching in a neighboring state for almost 10 years, but as a result of her husband's job transfer and the subsequent move it required, she had needed to find a new teaching position. Being an experienced teacher, she felt she should know all of the information being presented by the program facilitators. In fact, she resented being required to attend this program. It was when the district's director of student services brought up the topic of School Intervention Assistance Teams that her feeling of confusion set in. The concept of a problem-solving team designed to help teachers with hard-to-teach or hard-to-manage students sounded like a great idea. Could her previous school district have had this type of program and she just hadn't known about it?

That evening, she called a friend and teaching colleague from her previous school district. During their phone conversation, the friend expressed her opinion that the School Intervention Assistance Team sounded something like the Pupil Intervention Committee in her previous district. Mrs. Thompson had already considered this possibility, but had concluded that even though the processes shared similarities, these two teams were significantly different. The School Intervention Assistance Team in Mrs. Thompson's new district was a voluntary problem-solving team consisting of general education teachers who met during the school day to help teachers requesting assistance. Consulting the Pupil Intervention Committee in her old district was a mandatory step that teachers were required to take if they intended to refer a student for a special education evaluation. The committee was led by the school principal and was composed of special education personnel. All of the meetings of the Pupil Intervention Committee were held after school. Teachers were told that this was due to scheduling constraints, but most of the teachers believed this was a strategy designed to deter them from initiating the process.

Upon ending the phone call, Mrs. Thompson felt just as confused as ever. Later, as she was lying in bed before going to sleep, she reflected on the possibility that maybe she didn't know as much as she had thought she did. As she turned off the light beside her bed, she realized that to succeed in her new school district it would be important for her to learn about these new procedures and services.

VARIATIONS ON A THEME

Although fictitious, Mrs. Thompson's confusion is likely a reality for many teachers who change jobs and start out in new school districts. According to Truscott, Cohen, Sams, Sanborn, and Frank (2005), 86 percent of states either require or recommend prereferral intervention activities. This is true despite the fact that there are no federal mandates requiring them. Certainly, revisions to the Individuals with Disabilities Education Act and passage of the No Child Left Behind Act are major pieces of federal legislation that encourage early intervention for students who demonstrate academic difficulties. However, states currently remain free to decide whether or not to incorporate prereferral intervention processes into their education regulations.

One result of allowing this choice has been implementation practices that vary considerably across states, school districts within the same state, and even schools within the same district. Prereferral intervention activities are one of the most inconsistently applied processes in education, and variance can be found across multiple dimensions.

Some states require prereferral intervention activities, some recommend them, and others neither require nor recommend them. Where they are required or recommended, the names for the school-based teams formed to implement the prereferral process vary considerably. Consider these examples: Teacher Assistance Teams, Teacher Intervention Teams, Prereferral Intervention Teams, Student Assistance Teams, School Support Teams. In 25 states there is no standard term used for describing the prereferral process (Buck, Polloway, Smith-Thomas, & Cook, 2003).

In states that provide training for the prereferral process, it is most often the responsibility of local school districts. In some states, this training is the responsibility of a state education agency. Yet in a significant number of states, no training for completing the prereferral process is provided by anyone (Buck et al., 2003).

In the majority of states, general education teachers are responsible for implementing and leading the prereferral process. However, in several states special education teachers and administrators are assigned the primary responsibility for implementing the prereferral process. The composition and size of the teams responsible for completing prereferral activities, as well as the type of services they provide, vary widely even within the same state or school district.

Regardless of differences in title and design, most prereferral intervention activities share some common conceptual features. First, the process used is intended to be preventative in nature. More specifically, interventions are developed and implemented before a formal, special education evaluation is conducted. Second, the process uses an action-research model. Teams develop specific interventions that the referring teachers are expected to implement in their classroom and evaluate in terms of their effectiveness. Third, the intervention process is focused on enhancing the success of students and teachers in the general education setting and in the general education curriculum. Last, a team-based problem-solving approach is used. Team members review data on a referred student, hypothesize the causes that might explain the student's difficulties, and develop strategies to remediate those difficulties.

EDUCATIONAL LEADER'S ROLE

Having been a high school math and science supervisor, Ellen Santiago was thankful to have Jim Dalton as her mentor now. Ellen's first few weeks as an elementary school principal were going well. Having been a teacher at the secondary level for 10 years and then a subject area supervisor for 6 years, she felt very confident in her ability to serve as an instructional leader. However, her lack of experience at the elementary level and more specifically her lack of leadership at the building level had presented some challenges. Until this point, Jim's advice, accrued from 10 years of experience as an elementary principal, had helped her meet the challenges presented.

On this day, she received a memo from the district director of student personnel services, which stated that it was time for the school buildings to start the prereferral intervention team process. Ellen was familiar with the concept, but she had never been responsible for managing or leading the process. Naturally, she turned to her mentor for guidance on how to proceed. She picked up the phone and called Jim.

After exchanging the usual pleasantries, she mentioned the memo. The following is the rest of that conversation:

Jim: Yes, Ellen, I did receive that memo. I meant to mention to you the last time we spoke that this would be coming out. You have to be really careful with this one.

Ellen: Why is that?

Jim: The district is under scrutiny to lower the number of classified students. No one will put this in writing, but it is expected that the principals will force every evaluation to go through the prereferral intervention team so that we can keep it from going to a special education evaluation.

Ellen: What if a student really needs a special education evaluation?

Jim: I know this sounds wrong, but if you want to keep yourself out of trouble with the Central Office, you have to do everything you can to avoid that. Don't put this in writing, but make it clear to your staff that they have to refer all students to the prereferral intervention team. Also, put people you can control on the committee. I try to stack it with nontenured teachers. This way I can control the outcomes of the meetings.

Ellen: Jim, this doesn't sound right to me. I would be denying services to kids who may really need them. Besides that, I'm not really sure I can make accurate judgments on my own about who needs what.

Jim: That's why if I suspect a child may need a special education evaluation, I secretly talk to the parents and coach them on how to write a letter requesting it. The district has no choice but to consider those requests. I just hope that I don't get caught.

As Ellen hung up the phone, she thought to herself that there must be a better way. In fact, there are much more effective and efficient methods for conducting this process. Although prereferral intervention teams are common and schools devote considerable personnel resources and time to them, there remains a significant difference between these teams as they are described in research literature and as they operate in most schools.

As in Jim and Ellen's situation, political realities often contribute to how the prereferral process is implemented. However, even more significant is most educational leaders' lack of knowledge and skill as it relates to prereferral intervention activities. Research, experience, and discussion with colleagues have revealed that most school administrators do not receive any formal training in the management and leadership of prereferral intervention programs. It is part of neither their formal preservice coursework nor their in-service training. Instead, they frequently rely on past experience or the advice of colleagues. But neither of these sources of information is usually grounded in research on effective prereferral intervention practices.

Administrative support, especially by building-level leaders, has been cited by several researchers as the single most important factor influencing the effectiveness of prereferral intervention activities (Bahr & Kovaleski, 2006; Kovaleski & Glew, 2006; Kruger, Struzziero, Watts, & Vacca, 1995). Considering the significant role that educational leaders play in the success or failure of prereferral intervention activities, this makes the current situation even more troublesome. It is the intent of this book to bridge the gap between current practice and research literature.

It is not the direct involvement of school administrators as members of prereferral intervention teams that is most important. In fact, a substantial body of evidence supports the assertion that teachers express greater satisfaction with collaborative prereferral intervention activities when school administrators are not members of the team (Rafoth & Foriska, 2006; Safran & Safran, 1996). What, then, is the importance of school administrators in making prereferral intervention activities effective?

One frequently overlooked aspect of prereferral intervention activities is the fact that all of the names given to the process include the word *team*, which signifies that these activities are supported by a team process. Thus, to achieve effectiveness in this area, educational leaders must have the knowledge and skill required to design, establish, and support effective problem-solving teams. The school administrator's critical role is to create the conditions that will support the effectiveness of prereferral intervention teams. Rather than being directly involved in the team's activities, educational leaders must focus their efforts on creating a context within their schools that increases the likelihood that these teams will operate efficiently and effectively.

Chapters 2–5 provide the educational leader with a means for accomplishing this task. More specifically, they provide a sequential, four-phase model designed to result in effective prereferral intervention teams. Chapter 6 then focuses on methods for evaluating the effectiveness of a prereferral intervention program. Chapter 7 presents the potential connection between the Response to Intervention model for identifying learning disabilities and prereferral intervention teams. Resource A provides educational leaders with a systematic plan for implementing the steps described in Chapters 2–5.

CONCLUSION

The majority of states and school districts require some form of prereferral intervention teams. Even though the structure and processes of these teams vary widely, these teams share some defining characteristics. Unfortunately, they frequently share a significant discrepancy between how they are described in research literature and how they are implemented in schools. This is due in part to educational leaders' lack of knowledge and skills in designing, managing, and leading these teams. Because the support of educational leaders is critical to the success of prereferral intervention teams, this is a situation that must be rectified if these teams are to be effective.

CHAPTER TWO

The Analysis and Decision-Making Phase

The idea is to make decisions and act on them—to decide what is important to accomplish, to decide how something can best be accomplished, to find time to work at it, and to get it done.

—Karen Kakascik

After getting off the phone with Jim, Ellen decided to look up prereferral intervention activities in her district policy manual. As she read the district's policies and procedures for prereferral intervention activities, Ellen began to feel a sense of panic. She read the information a second time in hopes that maybe she had missed something the first time. Surely there must be more guidance than references to the state code and some vague statements about roles and responsibilities for completing the process. What type of student problems should teachers refer to the prereferral intervention team? How frequently should the team meet? Should the meetings be before, during, or after school? Does the team have the authority to modify district programs and practices?

These are just a few of the questions Ellen had hoped to find answers to in the district policy manual.

Being someone who takes action to resolve her inner conflicts, Ellen decided to visit the research library at her local university in search of answers. Knowing that she had to have a prereferral intervention team in her school was one thing. Determining how much time and effort to put into this process was quite another. With the limited time she and her staff had, she needed to determine if prereferral intervention activities were worth a significant investment of time and energy. With the assistance of a research librarian, she located numerous studies on this topic. As she read them, she made note of the costs and benefits associated with prereferral intervention teams.

COSTS AND BENEFITS

The first benefit Ellen identified from her review of the research reminded her of her friend Janet Anderson, a second-grade teacher. She remembered how several years ago, Janet struggled with a decision. It was early November, and Janet didn't know what to do about her student Alex. As she described it at the time, he consistently demonstrated difficulties paying attention in class. Often during Janet's lessons, Alex daydreamed or doodled on the covers of his books. In a conversation with Ellen over a cup of coffee, Janet explained how she had repeatedly reprimanded Alex for his behavior and had communicated her concerns to his parents. Ellen remembered how Janet struggled with the decision of whether to refer him to the special education team so that he could be evaluated for a disability. Janet eventually did decide to make the referral. She concluded that it was the most prudent action she could take to help Alex.

Ellen remembered how Janet described what occurred next. Over the course of the next two months, Alex was evaluated by a school psychologist and a learning disability specialist, and his family was interviewed by a school social worker. Eventually, they determined that he was eligible for special education. As Janet described it, according to the school psychologist, a boy with Alex's intellectual ability should have been performing at a much higher level. He was identified as having a learning disability and was placed in a combination of pullout replacement classes and general education classes.

Even though she had never said so, Ellen knew that Janet struggled with the outcomes resulting from that decision because she would occasionally tell Ellen about recent news that Alex's current teachers had shared with her. As it turned out, over the course of the next three years, Alex's program remained the same. He remained in a small-group setting receiving instruction from a special education teacher for several of his subject areas. In fifth grade, he was reevaluated by the special education team. Ellen remembered how concerned Janet had been by the results of Alex's reevaluation. According to the testing, the gap between his performance and his peers' performance had actually grown. He continued to perform significantly below grade level in reading and math, and there had been less than one half of a year of growth for each year that he had been in the special education program.

Believing that they needed to take intensive action to close this gap, the team decided to place Alex in a self-contained special education classroom. He received all of his academic instruction in this classroom and was only in the general education program for lunch and "specials" (e.g., art, music, physical education). In addition, counseling had been added to his program to assist him with the poor self-image he had developed. Ellen felt for Janet because she knew Janet questioned whether she had made the correct decision for Alex.

Ellen's review of the research literature caused her to question that decision as well. What if Alex never really had a learning disability? What if he did not perform well in Janet's class because of other factors such as classroom, instructional, or school practices? What if the evaluations administered by the psychologist and the learning disability specialist would have found similar results for many other children who never were referred to special education? What would have happened to Alex if Janet had made changes to her classroom and instructional practices and he had remained in the regular education program? Unfortunately for Alex, Ellen knew no one would ever know the answers to these questions. One thing Ellen did suspect was that if Janet had had access to and utilized an effective prereferral intervention program, the chance of an inappropriate special education referral would have been reduced.

Current practices in special education can be characterized as inconsistent and problematic. From referral to program planning, each phase of the process is flawed. Students are being referred for evaluations in increasing numbers (Bahr & Kovaleski, 2006), and the reasons for these referrals frequently have less to do with the student's classroom functioning than with the teacher, the school, or other variables. Once referred, students are almost automatically tested, which is often done with instruments that are technically inadequate. Upon completion of this testing, the vast majority of these students are placed in special education. Frequently, the basis of this determination is the inconsistent and inherently problematic discrepancy formula used to define learning disabilities.

The first benefit that Ellen saw in her review of the research was that prereferral intervention teams offer an alternative to this traditional model of referral. Because prereferral activities target interventions at the point prior to initial referral, they can reduce inappropriate referrals to special education (Buck, Polloway, Smith-Thomas, & Cook, 2003; Flugum & Reschly, 1994; Fuchs, Fuchs, Bahr, Fernstrom, & Stecker, 1990).

The second benefit Ellen identified reminded her of the budget meeting she had attended last winter. The superintendent and business administrator had summoned all of the administrators to the Board of Education office. They had spent hours identifying additional programs and services that had to be cut from the budget because the overall costs proposed were excessive. It had seemed that everyone but the Special Education Department had major funding reductions. In fact, this department had received a significant increase in its allocation of funds. As the director of student services had explained several times, all of the work this department did was required by federal law. Ellen vividly remembered the director's comment: "If you don't want us to spend so much money, stop sending us so many kids." Although this comment had been made in the heat of the moment, Ellen could not help wondering if it contained an element of truth.

School personnel spend many hours on each special education evaluation—preparing, testing, analyzing, writing, presenting results—all of which cost time and money. These costs are frequently high because the individuals doing the work are highly specialized (and thus are usually paid more) and the work is done by more than one person. Furthermore, when these professionals are involved in the student evaluation process, their time cannot be spent consulting with teachers or providing direct service to students.

When you consider the current fiscal climate, the high cost of conducting a student evaluation, and the loss of services resulting from the tasks required, it becomes apparent that referrals for special education evaluations should be done only when obvious and appropriate. Effective and systematic prereferral intervention activities have demonstrated the ability to provide cost savings due to fewer inappropriate special education referrals (Bahr, Whitten, Dieker, Kocarek, & Manson, 1999; Fuchs et al., 1990).

Ellen was surprised that she had not thought about the third benefit of an effective prereferral intervention program. Janet and Alex came to mind once again. She remembered Janet's frustration with the amount of time it had taken for the school psychologist, learning disability specialist, and social worker to complete their evaluations. It had taken almost three months from the time Janet had decided to request the evaluation to the time the special education team had made a determination of Alex's eligibility. Although Ellen wasn't sure, it made sense to her that during those three months, Janet hadn't done much that was different to help Alex. If he had been struggling already and Janet hadn't known what else to do, wouldn't Alex have continued to fall further behind his classmates during that time?

The special education process from initial referral to eligibility determination has timelines. Due to their workload, those responsible for completing the process often complete their tasks near or at the end of those timelines. During that waiting period, the student typically does not receive any additional or different services. By initiating the referral, a teacher such as Janet has already indicated that she does not believe she has the knowledge or skills to appropriately meet the student's needs. Thus, the student continues to struggle, falling farther behind his or her classmates. A coordinated system of prereferral intervention enables educators to respond in a timely manner to students who are experiencing difficulties meeting the social and academic demands of school (O'Shaugnessy, Lane, Gresham, & Beebe-Frankenberger, 2003). Although not based on the same types of data as an individualized evaluation conducted by a multidisciplinary evaluation team, prereferral intervention activities provide teachers and students with timely and responsive assistance.

Ellen found these three benefits important, but it was the fourth one that really got her excited. Up until this point, she had only considered the benefits of prereferral intervention activities for students. She hadn't thought about the fact that these collaborative problem-solving activities could improve teachers' skills and attitudes as well. Of course, it made sense that when teachers get together to systematically conduct brainstorming activities and generate solutions to immediate problems, it would be an excellent form of job-embedded staff development. An effective system of prereferral intervention activities could improve teachers' effectiveness in working with student problems in general. It also made sense to Ellen that as teachers became more effective in working with student problems, their attitudes toward students who experience academic and behavioral problems might become more positive. These improvements in teachers' skills and attitudes through collaborative problem-solving would certainly help her establish the inclusive, collaborative professional learning community she desired for her school.

Although Ellen was excited by the potential benefits of effective prereferral intervention programs, she knew there would be costs. Her synthesis of the literature made it clear that effectively organized prereferral intervention activities place high demands on the referring teacher. If it is to be successful, a systematic, structured program requires the referring teacher to expend time and effort. With the demands already placed on them, would the teachers on Ellen's staff be willing and able to meet these additional requirements?

Effective prereferral intervention activities also shift the focus from the disabilities residing within the student to the analysis of the broader classroom context. Ellen wondered how the teachers on her staff would react to this change in focus. Would they feel threatened? She also wondered how they might react if she changed expectations for the ownership of the problem. With the special education evaluation process, teachers could transfer ownership of a student's problems to special education personnel. But with effective prereferral intervention activities, the expectation is that teachers will participate in a set of problem-solving activities designed to assist them with helping a student succeed.

After reading and reviewing the literature, Ellen was left with a piece of paper divided into two columns. On one side were the benefits, and on the other side the costs.

Example Cost–Benefit Analysis

Benefits	Costs
Reductions in the number of inappropriate special education referrals.	Time and energy demands on the referring teacher.
Reduced costs for special education services.	Threatening nature of shift in focus for source of student's problem.
Timely and responsive interventions.	Frustration associated with change in expectations for problem-ownership.
Enhanced teacher skills and attitudes.	
More inclusive, collaborative school environment.	

As Ellen reflected on the costs and benefits, she realized that to receive the benefits from prereferral intervention activities, high-quality implementation of a systematic, structured program would be required. She agreed with Kovaleski and Glew's (2006) conclusion that poor implementation of effective prereferral practices generates no significant difference in student performance. She was confronted with a decision. Considering the cultural, structural, and political realities of her school and district, could she initiate and sustain a high-quality prereferral intervention program?

As Ellen drove home, she reflected on this question. Being the school's new principal presented both challenges and opportunities. As she assessed her situation, she saw that maintaining the status quo would be the safer action to take. If she initiated changes in the prereferral intervention program and they didn't succeed, her staff might lose confidence in her. Then again, while she was still relatively new, her staff might be more receptive to change. In private conversations with the staff, they had expressed to her the need to revitalize the school's programs. They appeared to expect some changes as the result of the change in school leadership.

What about the other elementary school principals? How would they react to her making changes to her school's prereferral intervention program? She reasoned that each school was required to have the same programs, but they did not have to be run in the same way. Jim's school had a gifted and talented program and a basic skills program that were both different than the programs at Ellen's school. She concluded that if she didn't make a big deal about the changes, then the other elementary principals probably would not be upset with her actions.

Jim had warned her about the central office's position on this issue. She certainly didn't want to make changes that would be met with disapproval by the director of student services or the superintendent of schools. However, the outcomes that they desired appeared to be aligned with the benefits of the types of programs she had read about in the research literature. Because no training or guidance had been provided in the process of planning, managing, and leading prereferral intervention programs, the bottom line for these administrators seemed to be the outcomes achieved. How Ellen achieved those outcomes appeared to be left to her discretion.

Last, Ellen thought about her own needs. She already felt overwhelmed by everything she needed to learn about elementary schools. She was working 12-hour days and coming in on the weekends trying to meet the demands of her new position. Taking on something else at this time seemed like it might be more than she could handle. However, she had applied for and accepted this position because she had become increasingly convinced that early intervention was critical. As a secondary school educator she had become frustrated by how difficult it was to improve the performance of at-risk learners who had struggled for most of their school careers. Perhaps making changes to her current school's prereferral intervention program would further energize her and give her that sense of purpose she was searching for.

After sleeping on it, Ellen made the decision to put the time and effort into developing an effective prereferral intervention program in her school. She knew it would likely be a difficult journey, but she believed that the benefits outweighed the costs and the changes required were feasible.

Ellen's journey to reach this decision is an example of the type path that a school administrator confronted with a similar decision should take. Reviewing the costs and benefits of implementing or revising a prereferral intervention program forces the educational leader to evaluate whether it is an effective use of time and energy. And even if the benefits appear to outweigh the costs, it is important to know whether the implementation or revision of a systematic, structured prereferral intervention program is feasible. Every school and district has existing cultural, political, and structural characteristics. If these characteristics combine to make it unlikely that change will succeed, then it would be unwise to invest significant time and energy in this area. Instead, effort should be focused on influencing changes so that eventually they will support a high-quality prereferral intervention program.

If you are in a situation like Ellen's, it is important to think about your personal circumstances, as she did. Change is often a difficult, challenging journey. Meeting this challenge requires time, effort, and conviction. Do you have the motivation? Can you invest the time and energy to see the change through? If not, it may not be the right time to attempt this change. Assuming that the benefits outweigh the costs and program changes are feasible, then it is likely a good time to invest energy and effort into prereferral intervention program changes. The next step is to determine the tasks to be accomplished by the prereferral intervention team.

ESTABLISHING AND ANALYZING THE TASK

Having made the decision to invest the time and energy necessary to create a high-quality prereferral intervention program, Ellen knew her next step was to decide what the program should accomplish. Her experience in leading school teams had led her to believe that this step was critical because it would guide every action she took from this point forward. As a result, she spent several days reviewing students' standardized test scores, grades, attendance data, discipline reports, and special education classification rates. She also talked informally with teachers about their most pressing student concerns and the methods that they were using to address them. Last, she talked with the special education personnel assigned to her building to get their views on this issue. After mentally synthesizing this information, she sat down at her desk and wrote out the following statement:

Our school's prereferral intervention team will serve as a systematic, collaborative, problem-solving team that all of the teachers can access to help them create and implement interventions that will eliminate or mitigate student's learning, behavior, health, or social-emotional problems. This team will not serve as a mechanism for delaying the provision of needed services to students with disabilities.

Satisfied with her initial attempt at defining the task, she proceeded to think about how those receiving or reviewing the outcomes of the prereferral intervention team would assess the quality of the services it provided. The groups she considered were teachers, students, and district administrators. After some time spent reflecting, she wrote:

Teachers accessing this service will believe that they have been provided with effective ideas that can be realistically implemented in their classrooms. District administrators will see a decrease in the number of referrals to special education, with a high percentage of those referred being eligible for classification.

Most important, students of the teachers accessing this service will demonstrate improved academic performance and classroom conduct that generalizes across time and settings.

Feeling clear about the nature of the task, Ellen proceeded to analyze the significant variables that might impact successful task completion. She remembered from a seminar she had attended that the effectiveness of every school-based work team is a joint function of three variables: (1) the level of effort that group members collectively put forth in carrying out the task, (2) the amount of knowledge and skill that members bring to bear on the group's task, and (3) the appropriateness of the strategies used by the group in its work. In that seminar, the presenter had emphasized that all three of these variables are significant to some degree in most schools and districts. However, in each particular situation, usually one or two are more significant for group effectiveness. Focusing on which of these factors are most critical to the successful completion of the task would help Ellen improve the results from the limited time she had to spend on designing and managing the school's prereferral intervention team.

Clearly, the quantity and quality of skills and knowledge that team members possess would make a significant difference in the team effectively completing the task at hand. Similarly, the appropriateness of the strategies used by the team would also be important. Although effort is always important, Ellen believed that it would not be as critical as the other two variables. She concluded that as a result of this analysis she needed to pay careful attention to the composition of the prereferral intervention team and the team's norms about their performance processes. She was not going to neglect the importance of the team's efforts; she just wasn't going to spend as much time on this variable.

The process that Ellen went through to establish and analyze the task is the same process that any educational leader should go through in designing a school's prereferral intervention team. First, the educational leader must describe the task that the prereferral intervention team is expected to accomplish. This description should be as specific and concrete as possible. Although Ellen's task description is fictitious, it is one that is grounded in research and theory on prereferral intervention teams. However, it is neither the only nor the best possible description of such a team's task. As the educational leader, you must analyze your situation and develop a description of the task that is specific to your school or district needs.

Next, the educational leader must determine who will receive or review the outcomes of the services that the prereferral intervention team provides. How will these people assess the quality of the services provided? In Ellen's situation, three common "clients" of a school's prereferral intervention team were identified. Teachers and students would always be clients, but are district administrators important clients in your situation as well? Is anyone else an important client in your school or district?

The educational leader must then evaluate the relative importance of effort, knowledge, skill, and performance strategies to the team's successful completion of the task. If any of these variables are more important than others, then the implications of this fact must be considered when designing and managing the team. Like Ellen, your analysis of the task is likely to lead you to conclude that knowledge, skills, and performance strategies are more important variables than effort in the success of a prereferral intervention team. This conclusion should have a significant impact on how you plan and prepare for your school or district's team.

ESTABLISHING AUTHORITY

After establishing and analyzing the prereferral intervention team's tasks, Ellen turned her attention to the topic of authority. More specifically, she pondered what her role should be in relation to this team. Her initial thought was that she would serve as the team leader, which would provide her with an excellent opportunity to exercise her instructional leadership skills. After some additional reflection on this decision, however, she decided against being a standing team member, let alone the team leader. The type of collaborative problem-solving activities she wanted the team to engage in might not happen if she were to regularly attend team meetings. Ellen reasoned that her presence as the school administrator might inhibit open discourse. Furthermore, teachers may not want to bring problems to the team out of fear of being evaluated or appearing less competent in front of someone in authority. Once the teachers began to accept and trust her, then she could assume the role of a team member. For now, the team was going to have to be self-managing and she was going to have to provide the supports necessary for the team to be effective. She would attend team meetings when the team members decided that her presence would be valuable.

Having made the decision not to serve as a core team member, Ellen analyzed the task demands to determine the authority that the team members would need to complete their task effectively. First, they would need to be able to call on the knowledge and skills of other staff members for solving various problems. If they could schedule prereferral intervention team meetings without interrupting instruction or requiring a substitute teacher, team members could request the attendance of any staff member in the building at these meetings. If a substitute teacher would be required for a staff member to be able to provide a service to a student, then Ellen would have to approve the action first.

Second, team members would likely need to make curricular and instructional decisions for students. As long as the decision would not negatively impact other classes or violate any district or school policies, the team would be free to make those decisions. However, if the proposed intervention impacted other programs or violated any policy, then Ellen would need to have final approval.

Third, it was likely that some of the solutions generated by the team would require the expenditure of school funds. Ellen decided that if the funds needed were less than the amount typically provided by the petty cash fund, the team did not need her prior approval. However, any expenditure over that threshold would require her advance approval.

Ellen concluded that given the cultural, political, and structural realities of the school and district, this level of authority could be provided. Furthermore, she believed that staff members would be both willing and able to function at this level of authority. Her process was the same one that any educational leader should undertake as part of initiating or revising their school or district's prereferral intervention team process.

Concern that the presence of the school administrator will inhibit open discourse has led some researchers to advocate against having the principal serve as a team member. Askamit and Rankin (1993) caution that the presence of administrators on prereferral intervention teams may result in team members deferring to the "expert" and thus not engaging as extensively in the problem-solving process. Furthermore, Askamit and Rankin speculate that administrator involvement may result in teachers being less willing to bring problems to the team for fear of appearing incompetent. In addition, according to Sindelar, Griffin, Smith, and Watanabe (1992), teachers express greater satisfaction with collaborative prereferral teams when principals are not team leaders.

On the other hand, a principal's support for prereferral intervention teams appears to be a necessary condition for successful team functioning. Kruger, Struzziero, Watts, and Vacca (1995) state that administrative support is one organizational factor that has been consistently identified as being related to successful collaborative problem solving. Due to their ability to influence the school's climate and resources, principals are arguably the most important supporters of problem-solving teams (Kovaleski, 2002).

Current thought about the school administrator's role as it relates to prereferral intervention teams is that, although principal support is viewed as critical for successful team functioning, principal participation is not. It is important for educational leaders to be aware of the potential positive and negative effects of their involvement in these teams. When deciding which role they will assume, educational leaders must be clear about their desired impact. If they choose to become team members or leaders, then they must be strategic about facilitating an atmosphere of acceptance, trust, and open and honest communication.

CONCLUSION

The first phase for revising or implementing a prereferral intervention team is analysis and decision making. The steps of this Phase 1 are outlined in Figure 2.1.

Figure 2.1   Phase 1: Analysis and Decision Making

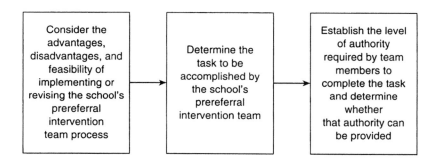

Within this phase, the educational leader should carefully consider the costs, benefits, and feasibility of making changes to a school or district's prereferral intervention program. Assuming that the benefits outweigh the costs and it is feasible to proceed, the educational leader must decide which task the team will be charged with achieving. Careful consideration of the nature of this task will require the educational leader to determine the level and type of authority that team members will require if they are to be effective. Having conducted this analysis and made the necessary decisions, the educational leader is ready to progress to the planning and preparation phase of prereferral intervention team development. This topic is the subject of Chapter 3.

C H A P T E R   T H R E E

The Planning and Preparation Phase

Failing to plan is planning to fail.

—Alan Lakein

As the educational leader, Ellen's primary objective in the planning and preparation phase is to make sure that the prereferral intervention team is appropriately designed and has a supportive school context. To achieve these objectives, she must analyze, select, and provide structures that will make it possible for the team to achieve high levels of performance. Let us now return to Ellen's decisions and actions as she prepares to launch her school's prereferral intervention team.

Ellen felt drained by the energy she had put into analyzing and making decisions related to her school's prereferral intervention process. Yet she also felt excited and satisfied by the quality of work she had just completed. After taking a walk around the school, she once again sat down at her desk. Staring out the window, she reflected on what her next steps should be. She reflected on previous team-based initiatives she had experienced that had failed miserably. A common theme that emerged from her reflection was that those responsible for initiating the teams never seemed to have done the careful planning or advanced preparation necessary for the team to be successful. It struck Ellen that this common mistake had been made by leaders before the team had even met for the first time. A result was that it became impossible for teams she had served on to succeed despite their best efforts and intentions. Ellen resolved not to let this happen to her prereferral intervention team initiative.

She thought back to the analysis and decision making she had completed. She concluded that there were four areas she had to plan and prepare for before the prereferral intervention team met. These areas were an extension of the work she had recently completed. Her first step would be to determine the composition of the prereferral intervention team.

DETERMINING GROUP COMPOSITION

Over dinner that evening, Ellen discussed the issue with her husband. They agreed that the composition of the team would have a direct and significant impact on the amount of knowledge and skill that the team members could apply to their collaborative problem-solving activities. Together, Ellen and her husband hashed out the criteria that she would use in selecting prereferral intervention team members. First, she would determine who among the staff had the necessary skills and training to effectively serve as members of the team. She took out a piece of paper and listed the staff members and their areas of expertise.

Example Team Composition Chart

Staff Member	Expertise
Jodie Sharpe	special education teacher
Donna Walters	guidance counselor
Holly Greene	school nurse
Cheryl Davis	basic skills teacher/reading specialist
Tom Edwards	school psychologist
Rebecca Jones	fourth-grade teacher

Staff Member	Expertise
Kristine Sampson	second-grade teacher
Leah Hampson	speech therapist
Kelly Bennert	third-grade teacher
Sandy Smith	kindergarten teacher
Alan Santawaso	fifth-grade teacher

Ellen realized that, although each of these individuals could potentially contribute to the prereferral intervention team, a group of this size would lead to problems. It was simply too large considering the need to make decisions and coordinate activities. She wanted the team to consist of six to eight staff members. Therefore, she looked at her list again and decided that some of the people could serve as consultants to the team when their expertise might be beneficial. For example, not every case would require the expertise provided by Holly Greene. As the school nurse, she could be asked to participate in collaborative problem-solving activities when the problem related to a student health concern. The same was true for Leah Hampson. When the problem related to a student's speech or language difficulties, Leah could serve as a member of the team.

Having gotten the potential core group size down to nine, Ellen decided to apply a second criterion: those selected must have at least moderate levels of collaborative skills. Experience had taught Ellen that some school staff members have little competence in the skill of working collaboratively with others. Furthermore, she had painfully experienced the reality that even one or two such individuals could significantly interfere with a team's ability to bring its members' talents and expertise to bear on the task. It was for this reason that she rejected her husband's idea to ask for volunteers from those on the initial list. The composition of the team was too important to be left to self-selection. Thus, Ellen looked at the list again and eliminated Tom Edwards and Kristine Sampson. Even though they were talented individuals with a great deal of knowledge and skill, they were not effective at working with colleagues in group settings.

Ellen was fairly satisfied with the names on this narrowed-down list. As a final check, she wanted to make sure the group had a good balance between homogeneity and heterogeneity. She felt that if the team members were too alike, they might get along well but not have the diversity necessary for generating creative solutions to the problems presented. On the other hand, if they were to diverse, they might struggle to understand one another's point of view. Ellen reviewed her list and felt that the experience, professional training, and personality of the members ensured an appropriate balance of talents and perspectives. She had finalized the list of seven members that would serve on her school's prereferral intervention team.

An educational leader planning and preparing for the implementation or revision of a prereferral intervention team should follow a process similar to Ellen's. First, the educational leader must review his or her list of staff members to determine those who have high levels of task-relevant expertise. In this case, such expertise includes strong knowledge of curriculum and instruction, excellent classroom management skills, varied classroom assessment techniques, and the ability to differentiate or individualize instruction. Of course, making this distinction requires that the educational leader possess accurate knowledge of each staff member's talents and skills.

After generating the initial list, the educational leader must determine which of those individuals also have at least moderate levels of collaborative skills. More specifically, which of the staff members on the initial list have demonstrated the ability to communicate effectively with parents and staff, possess a supportive personality, and have both the interest and ability to assist colleagues? Regardless of knowledge and skill, anyone who does not have at least moderate levels of collaborative skills should not be a core member of a school's prereferral intervention team. The interpersonal skills required to be an effective and helpful collaborator are at the core of the effectiveness of the problem-solving activities that the team will be expected to conduct.

The third step that the educational leader must take is to determine the optimal group size. Dysfunction tends to occur in large groups. Among other concerns, members of large groups often have difficulty making decisions and coordinating activities. Research supports the advantages of using groups that are slightly smaller than the task requires (Hackman, 2002). Thus, when forming a prereferral intervention team, the educational leader should make the core team no larger than absolutely necessary for accomplishing the task. When their particular expertise and training are deemed appropriate and valuable, specialists should be invited to serve as ad hoc members of the team. Using the previously generated list of staff members who have both task-relevant expertise and at least moderate collaborative skills, the educational leader must then select the appropriate number of members for the team.

In general, the wider the variety of professional training and expertise among team members, the greater the range of interventions and support that can be offered to the referring teacher. However, the dynamics among the members of the team will impact the team's ability to utilize members' talents and skills. Therefore, the educational leader should review the composition of the team to ensure that it is diverse enough to provide a variety of talents and perspectives, but similar enough that members can successfully understand and coordinate with one another. If the balance is not appropriate, the educational leader must go back to the original list and make the necessary adjustments.

Criteria for Prereferral Intervention Team Composition

- Members have high task-relevant expertise.
- Members have at least moderate levels of collaborative skills.
- Group size is limited to no more than the number necessary for task completion.
- The group has an appropriate balance between homogeneity and heterogeneity.

DESIGNING AND COMMUNICATING THE TASK

With the purpose and function of the school's prereferral intervention team established, how could Ellen motivate her staff to invest a significant amount of time and energy into this process?

More specifically, Ellen identified her challenge as designing and communicating the task to team members so that it would be perceived as both clear and motivating.

It seemed logical to Ellen that the nature of the team's task would affect the amount of effort team members would put into completing their work. If they found their task exciting, fulfilling, or otherwise rewarding, then a norm encouraging high effort would likely emerge. Ellen reflected on the task from the point of view of potential team members, which led her to the conclusion that if she were a member of this team, the task would be motivating if it possessed three characteristics.

First, to put forth significant amounts of time and energy, team members would have to perceive the task as being meaningful. From Ellen's point of view, a meaningful task required team members to use a variety of skills and talents, produce a tangible outcome as a result of their work, and have a significant impact on the lives of others.

Due to the problem-solving, communication, and decision-making skills required by the nature of the prereferral intervention team's work, Ellen felt confident that team members would engage in activities that challenged and stretched their skills and abilities. Furthermore, the fact that they would complete an intervention plan from initial problem solving through to plan evaluation meant that their work would result in a tangible outcome. Most important, Ellen felt that the new emphasis placed on the team assisting colleagues with students who are difficult to teach and manage would make a substantial impact. From what she had learned about her staff, she knew that they would consider the work meaningful if the overarching purpose was collaborative problem solving. She was confident that the prereferral intervention team's task would be perceived by team members as meaningful.

Ellen believed that a second critical characteristic of motivating tasks is the level of autonomy given to those working on the task. She intuitively sensed that as the team's autonomy level increased, feelings of responsibility for the outcomes of the team's work would also increase. In planning the group's work, Ellen wanted to give the team members substantial freedom, independence, and discretion for scheduling their activities and carrying out their work. Her decision not to serve as a permanent member of the team was one factor that could increase the team's autonomy. However, Ellen knew that there were limits to the autonomy she could provide. Not only did she have to be clear about the outcomes the team was to achieve, but the district required that certain forms be used and specific information be reported annually. These were nonnegotiable items that the team would have to accept and work with.

The final characteristic that Ellen believed was necessary for a task to be motivating was feedback. She thought about her experiences as a basketball player and coach. The outcome of each game provided players and coaches with feedback about the effectiveness of their efforts. Not only was the feedback direct and clear, it could be used to improve the team's future efforts. Ellen wanted to make sure the school's prereferral intervention team received similar types of feedback about its efforts. She concluded that the results of each intervention plan could serve as valuable ongoing feedback to the team.

Now that Ellen was comfortable with the motivational properties of the team's task, she turned her attention to providing clarity about the parameters of the performance situation. She had learned from experience that developing appropriate strategies for completing a task required team members to have a clear and complete understanding of their situation. After careful thought, she concluded that she would need to be clear with the team members about the requirements and constraints that could limit their options. In other words, she had to determine what the team must always do and never do as it worked toward task completion. Ellen decided to make two lists.

The team must always . . .

>   allow the referring teacher to select the ideas to be implemented for intervention,
>
>   maintain appropriate confidentiality of students' records and information,
>
>   notify and attempt to include parents and students (when appropriate) in team meetings,
>
>   use the required district forms and keep the data that must be reported to the district's central office,
>
>   attempt to generate solutions that can be implemented by the classroom teachers in their classrooms,

seek prior approval from the principal if a substitute teacher is required or a student will be denied a service due to a staff member attending a prereferral intervention team meeting.

The team must never . . .

allow the traditional disciplinary roles of staff members to take precedence over the problem-solving activities of the team,

view the problem as residing exclusively within the student,

place blame on any individual for a student's behavior or learning challenges,

convey the message that doing more and different things for a student is considered above and beyond the call of duty,

make curricular or instructional decisions without the principal's approval that negatively impact the overall instructional program or violate school or district policy,

spend school funds without the principal's approval that exceed the amount provided by the petty cash fund.

A second aspect of making the performance situation clear was communicating to team members who would be using and reviewing the team's services. Furthermore, they needed to know the standards that would be used to assess the adequacy of their performance. Ellen divided this new list into two "consumers" of the team's services. One obvious group of would be the teachers who would initiate a referral to the team. From her days as a teacher, Ellen reasoned that teachers would assess the adequacy of the team's services by the alternatives they generated. She decided that quality alternatives would be those the teachers had not already attempted, were realistic for the teachers to implement, and would empower the students being referred. The second group of consumer would be those who would review the team's performance. In this case, Ellen knew that the district's central office would review the data provided by the prereferral intervention team to determine how many of the referrals resulted in special education evaluations. Even though Ellen didn't like it, she knew at this point that this criterion was a political reality. The prereferral intervention team needed to be aware of this fact in a tactful manner and would have to act accordingly.

Ellen took these steps to create a task that is likely to be perceived as being both clear and motivating. An educational leader who is preparing to implement or revise a prereferral intervention team should follow the same process. For the task to have the potential to motivate team members, it should require the use of a variety of members' skills and talents, the completion of a "whole" and identifiable piece of work, and the opportunity to make a significant and meaningful difference in the lives of those in the school community. Furthermore, the task must be designed to give team members substantial freedom, independence, and discretion for scheduling their task-completion activities and determining the procedures to be used in carrying them out. Last, appropriate feedback mechanisms must be built into the task so that the team will receive trustworthy feedback about the adequacy of its performance. If the task lacks any of these elements, the educational leader should redesign the task to include them.

For the task to be clear to prereferral intervention team members, they must understand the parameters within which they must work. The educational leader must make the constraints and requirements surrounding the team's performance situation clear. The team must know the limits defining what they must always and never do. In addition, they must know who will use and review the services they provide as well as the standards that will be used to assess the adequacy of the team's efforts. If the educational leader does not provide clear and complete information about the situation, the team may develop a way of proceeding that seems reasonable to its members but when executed turns out to be completely inappropriate.

Criteria for Making the Prereferral Intervention Team's Task Clear and Motivating

- The task requires team members to use a variety of skills and talents.
- The task requires team members to complete a "whole," identifiable piece of work.
- The potential outcome of the task is one that makes a significant, meaningful difference.
- The team has substantial autonomy related to carrying out task-completion strategies.
- The task has mechanisms built in so that the team will receive trustworthy feedback.
- The constraints and requirements of task-completion strategies have been identified.
- The individuals using and reviewing the group's services as well as the standards they will employ have been identified.

SCHOOL AND DISTRICT SUPPORTS

Ellen decided that unless her presence was requested, she was not going to be directly involved in the day-to-day functioning of the school's prereferral intervention team. Instead, she was going to focus her efforts on making sure the team had the supports it required to effectively complete its tasks. After a period of extended reflection, she decided that these necessary supports could be grouped into four categories:

- staff development and training
- data and information
- rewards and recognition
- material resources

Ellen had been part of groups that had both a good mix of staff members and the appropriate size, but hadn't succeeded because the school context had undermined the group's efforts. Because of those experiences, she reasoned that these four aspects of the school context would have to support and reinforce the team's efforts.

Ellen believed that, in general, the prereferral intervention team would have within its membership most of the knowledge and skill necessary for conducting effective collaborative problem-solving activities. However, she also knew there would be times when issues relating to a particular student would present the team members with challenges falling outside the scope of their collective knowledge and skill. When this occurred, team members would need to know where the relevant expertise exists within the school or district and how they should proceed to access those services. So Ellen proceeded to create a list of the names of various district specialists, a brief description of what they should be contacted for, and the best way to reach them. Because she was not an expert in this area, she decided to make an appointment to review the accuracy of this list with the school district's supervisor of special services.

Ellen was aware that the data and information collected by the school could be critical to the success of the prereferral intervention team. The data normally collected on school attendance, discipline referrals, academic performance, and student health could be valuable for the team as it planned appropriate strategies for assisting a teacher with a student. Without this data, the team might develop a strategy for addressing a challenging behavior or learning concern that, although seemed reasonable, turned out not to address the root cause of the problem. Ellen would never forget the time she had spent designing a remedial reading program for a student only to learn that he required eyeglasses. The student's father had passed away, and the mother did not have insurance. The school nurse was working with the student's mother to access the state program so the required eyeglasses could be obtained. The nurse knew about this issue, but assumed the principal had shared the information with Ellen. As it turned out, once the boy obtained the eyeglasses, he was able to read text without any remedial assistance. Ellen's "best guess" for attempting to solve this student's problem had been incorrect because she had lacked the necessary information. This experience had taught Ellen that school staff members needed to share information in a systematic manner if they were to effectively solve problems.

To improve the probability that the school's prereferral intervention team would generate viable alternatives and select appropriate strategies, Ellen knew she needed to make sure the data required by the team was readily available. She wondered how practical it would be for her to provide this data. In some cases, the necessary data might not exist or might be costly to obtain. Certainly, the psychiatric evaluation of a student presenting severe behavioral challenges would be valuable. However, Ellen's school could not afford this expense, and parents might not be willing to get the evaluation done on their own. In such a case, the team would need to know that it will have to make decisions based on imperfect or incomplete data. On the other hand, Ellen didn't want the team to be overwhelmed by excess or irrelevant information. Too much data and information could result in the team spending time and energy sifting through data they never needed in the first place. Ellen decided that she would design the process so that initially the team would only be provided with basic data, which would be gathered by the referring teacher and listed on the referral form. However, she would also make it a point to explain how and where other information could be obtained. Thus, the team members would have the responsibility to decide which additional data they required and then use the appropriate means for obtaining it.

Ellen had always been troubled by the reward systems employed by schools. Individuals have a tendency to engage in behaviors that are rewarded, and teachers are no different. Unlike in her husband's situation as a vice president in a large corporation, Ellen could not offer financial incentives. However, it had been her experience that most teachers understood this fact and were genuinely satisfied when their efforts were acknowledged. She knew that she would have to determine what the members of the prereferral intervention team valued as potential rewards. In addition to her observations, she contemplated the simplicity of simply asking the team members what they felt was important.

Ellen had also learned that something that seems like a positive attempt to reward effort could actually undermine the motivation of team members. As a supervisor, she had been responsible for forming a committee to improve the math and science scores of the middle and high schools in the district. To help the committee gain momentum, she had publicly praised it whenever possible. This was the case even when it was obvious that the committee wasn't making any progress. In fact, it never did complete a cohesive and strategic plan. Ellen diagnosed one of the reasons for the lack of completing the task as the minimal effort the committee members exerted. From this experience, she reasoned that acknowledging mediocre effort or poor performance would negatively influence the amount of effort that team members put into their future activities.

A second mistake she had made with this committee was recognizing individual effort for the completion of a group activity. The divisiveness and conflict that resulted from having done this was considerable. As she learned from committee members through private conversations, instead of focusing on excellent team performance, the members competed with one another for recognition. It was not about the group's success, but rather about competition for the spotlight. Regardless of the type of reward or recognition she would provide to the prereferral intervention team, Ellen was determined to keep the focus on team and not individual behavior.

Ellen believed that the saddest mistake leaders made when designing and managing school teams was not providing the group with the necessary material resources. Based on her experience, when a school team lacks the tools, equipment, space, or human resources necessary for task completion, performance inevitably suffers. This was the case even when the team had most, if not all, of the other aspects required for positive team performance securely in place. She vividly recalled being a member of a middle school interdisciplinary teaching team that had not had a regular meeting location. Even though they had wanted to use their common planning time effectively, they had often wasted a significant amount of time finding a location to meet.

Ellen knew that if she were going to avoid this problem, she would have to make certain that the team had appropriate space to use for its meetings. Furthermore, she would need to provide team members with release time to attend these meetings. When the meetings were scheduled to occur outside of school hours, she would have to find a means of providing compensation. Due to the scheduling and record keeping required, the team would require some clerical support. Last, Ellen knew that the team would likely generate solutions requiring specific materials and supplies, the acquisition of which she would have to enable by providing funds.

These material resource requirements presented a significant challenge for Ellen. To provide these resources to the prereferral intervention team, she would have to reallocate some of her budgeted funds and make some other activities lower fiscal priorities. However, she was certain that if the team members were not provided with the necessary resources, then commitment to the process would likely be minimal. Furthermore, frustration resulting from the additional expectations placed on team members would likely occur.

Imagine going to a landscaping center to select a new bush. You know where you will place the bush in your yard and the approximate color and size that you would like it to be. After spending a significant amount of time looking for the perfect bush, you finally make a selection. You bring it home, read the planting directions, and carefully follow them. However, once the bush is in the ground, you fail to water it. In addition, the soil you have planted it in is filled with clay. As a result, the bush dies within a week. This scenario mirrors the mistake made by an educational leader who designs, forms, and launches a team and then withdraws from team activities. Instead of simply hoping for success, the educational leader must reinforce the team by providing a supportive school context.

The educational leader who initiates or revises a prereferral intervention team must make sure that the team has the support of the school's educational, informational, and reward systems.

Furthermore, the team must have the material resources required to successfully complete its tasks.

The staff development system for the school and district must make available the training and technical assistance required by team members. If the educational leader has systematically composed the team of members with an appropriate mix of task-related skills, then the team will already possess a high degree of knowledge and skill. However, due to the challenging and unique nature of some of the problems presented, the team may require or benefit from outside expertise. So the team will need to know who in the school or district has the relevant knowledge and skills. Additionally, the team will need to know how to access these individuals for assistance.

The data management system of the school and district must make available to team members the information that they require. Otherwise, the strategies developed will be left to chance rather than guided by informed and competent data analysis. The educational leader must determine the basic information that team members need in order to conduct collaborative problem-solving activities and then make it possible for team members to access this data. It is imperative for the success of the team that team members be responsible for acquiring the necessary data. Providing the basic data as well as the means for accessing additional relevant data will avoid the problem of the team being provided with either too much or too little information.

The reward system of the school and district should provide recognition and reinforcement for excellent team performance. When the team's actions result in the members receiving something that they collectively value, it increases the probability they will repeat those same actions. For the motivational benefits of rewards to be realized, they must meet certain criteria. First, the reward or recognition must be contingent on demonstrated excellence by the team. Second, if a team is the unit doing the work, then the team must be the unit receiving the recognition or reward. Rewards or recognition following these two basic principles will greatly reinforce the motivational properties built into the task.

Finally, team members must not be overloaded by the prereferral intervention process. Meetings, paperwork, and adjustments in structure and curriculum all require both time and effort. If team members are not provided with the necessary resources, then their commitment to the process will be minimal or they may get frustrated by the additional expectations placed on them. The educational leader must determine the material resources required by the school's prereferral intervention team and then provide those resources.

School and District Supports for Prereferral Intervention Teams

- The sources of potentially valuable outside expertise have been identified.
- Team members have been made aware of how to access these potential resources.
- Team members are provided with the basic data that they will need in order to complete their tasks.
- The sources of potentially valuable additional data as well as how to access this information have been identified.
- Rewards or recognition for performance are contingent on excellent team performance.
- Rewards or recognition are focused on team and not individual performance.
- Rewards or recognition are of value to team members.
- The material resources required for excellent performance are provided to teams.

THE TEAM CHARTER

Ellen was impressed but slightly overwhelmed by the work she had just completed. She was confident that her efforts would result in her school's prereferral intervention team being well designed and functioning in a supportive school context. Yet how could she convey this information to the team members in a manner that would be both concise and easily understood? As she pondered this dilemma, she was reminded of the work she was doing for the local recreation soccer league. She had agreed to serve as a member of its board of trustees. In her role as a board member, she had been provided with a copy of the league's charter, which she had felt was very helpful to her in understanding the purpose, priorities, and procedures of the league. So she decided to create a similar type of charter for her school's prereferral intervention team (Figure 3.1).

Figure 3.1   Sample Prereferral Intervention Team Charter (a blank
charter can be found in Resource B #1)

Core Team Members	
Jodie Sharpe	Kelly Bennert
Donna Walters	Sandy Smith
Cheryl Davis	Alan Santawoso
Rebecca Jones	

Team's Task
Our school's prereferral intervention team will serve as a systematic, collaborative, problem-solving team that all of the teachers can choose to access in order to assist them with creating and implementing interventions designed to eliminate or mitigate student's learning, behavior, health, or social-emotional problems.

Effectiveness Criteria
Teachers accessing this service will believe that they have been provided with effective ideas that can be realistically implemented in their classrooms. District administration will see a decrease in the number of referrals to special education, with a high percentage of those being referred being eligible for classification. Most important, students of the teachers accessing this service will demonstrate improved academic performance and classroom conduct that generalizes across settings and time.

Task Parameters	
Must always do	Must never do
Allow the referring teacher to select the ideas to be implemented for intervention.	Allow the traditional disciplinary roles of staff members to take precedence over the problem-solving activities of the team.
Maintain appropriate confidentiality of student records and information.	View the problem as residing exclusively within the student.
When appropriate, notify and attempt to include parents and students in team meetings.	Place blame on any individual for a student's behavior or learning challenges.
Use the required district forms, and keep the data that must be reported to the district's central office.	Convey the message that doing more and different things for a student is considered above and beyond the call of duty.

Must always do	Must never do
Attempt to generate solutions that can be implemented by classroom teachers in their classrooms.	Make curricular or instructional decisions without the principal's approval that negatively impact the overall instructional program or violate school or district policy.
Seek prior approval from the principal if a substitute teacher is required or a student will be denied a service due to a staff member attending a prereferral intervention team meeting.	Spend school funds without the principal's approval that exceed the amount provided by the petty cash fund.

Educational Resources		
Name	Knowledge and skill	How to access
Holly Greene	School nurse	Ext. 212, Room 1
Leah Hampson	Speech and language specialist	Ext. 311, Room 2 (Mon., Thurs.)
Tom Edwards	School psychologist	Ext. 219, Room 16
Brandon Thompson	School social worker	Ext. 411, Central Office
Janet Evans	Reading specialist	Ext. 413, Central Office

Information Resources	
Type of data	Location
Attendance records	Main Office, Mrs. DeShanes
Health records	Nurse's Office, Mrs. Myers
Discipline records	Main Office, Mrs. Anderson
Students' cumulative records folders	Main Office, Mrs. DeShanes

Material Resources (clerical support, space, time, supplies, and materials)
The team may use the principal's conference room for all meetings. To use the room, schedule the meeting on the posted calendar.
A locked filing cabinet will be placed in the principal's conference room for the team to store meeting materials.
The team may ask Mrs. Anderson to conduct clerical tasks related to the team's activities.
The team may purchase materials for implementing interventions at a cost up to the threshold for petty cash requests. Any cost beyond that threshold will require prior written approval of the principal.

CONCLUSION

The second step that an educational leader who is considering revising or implementing a prereferral intervention team should take is planning and preparation. The steps of phase two are outlined in Figure 3.2.

Figure 3.2   Phase 2: Planning and Preparation

Within this phase, the educational leader should identify an appropriate composition for the team. In addition, the educational leader must review the team's task that was created in Phase 1 to determine how to communicate it to team members in a manner that is both clear and motivating. Last, the educational leader must examine the contextual supports required by the team to make sure that they will enhance and not hinder effective team performance. The work that has been described in Chapters 2 and 3 should ultimately lead to the creation of a prereferral intervention team charter. This charter will be shared with team members during the start-up phase of team development, which is the subject of Chapter 4.

CHAPTER FOUR

The Start-Up Phase

Let us watch well our beginnings, and results will manage themselves.

—Alexander Clark

Having planned and prepared for her school's prereferral intervention team, Ellen turned her attention to forming and building the group. She pondered what she could do when the team members met for the first time that would increase the probability that the group would work together effectively. She decided that there were four things she needed to do if the team was to begin with positive momentum. First, she needed to clarify with the team who were and were not the core members of the team. Second, she needed to make sure the team members understood the task to be completed as well as the desired outcomes. Third, she needed to lead the team members in developing positive group behavioral norms and assigning member roles. Fourth, she needed to provide the team members with the initial training they would need to complete their tasks.

TEAM BOUNDARIES

As a member of many different school and district teams, Ellen had experienced the problem of membership in a team not being clearly delineated. As a result of this lack of clarity, she and her fellow team members had not been certain who was and who was not a group member. Thus, they had struggled to work interdependently to complete the assigned task. Ellen's experience had led her to conclude that one primary reason for this lack of clarity was that staff members often were members of multiple teams. Some of these teams, such as grade-level, subject area, and interdisciplinary teams, were more established and permanent than the temporary teams formed to address specific school or district issues. Frequently, members of the temporary or less well-developed teams prematurely sought input for decisions or feedback on a product from others in the more established, permanent teams to which they also belonged. This often resulted in disagreement among team members as to how to proceed. Members became frustrated because the "outsiders" often did not fully understand the situation, nor were they going to be held accountable for the final outcomes. As a result of the ambiguity regarding group composition, team members often became frustrated and performance suffered.

To avoid this potential difficulty, Ellen decided to clearly define who was and was not a core member of the school's prereferral intervention team. Core members would be defined as those who shared responsibility for the completion of the group task; these individuals would be accountable for the final product or decision. By reviewing and explaining the section of the team charter that listed the team members, Ellen believed that she could make sure the group was certain who was a member of the team. In addition, when reviewing the team's task and the desired outcomes, she would link core team membership with accountability for producing the outcomes required.

TASK REDEFINITION

Another difficulty that Ellen had experienced as a member of many different teams was idiosyncratic interpretations of the team's task. Often the school administrator believed that the task was clearly understood once it had been explained. Yet this was rarely the case. The situation was especially problematic when the task had multiple or conflicting objectives. Ellen could remember how difficult this problem had been for the district committee charged with selecting a new superintendent of schools. The Board of Education had charged the group with selecting a candidate who met a vast number of criteria. However, the group had also been charged with completing this task in a very short time frame. The conflict between the quality of the decision and the speed by which it was to be made had never been discussed. Thus, the conflict had been neither resolved nor accepted by the committee as an issue that it would need to manage. As a result, the committee had rushed through the process of selecting a candidate who, in the end, lasted less than six months in the position.

Ellen decided that she would deal with questions of task definition in the prereferral intervention team's start-up meeting. She believed that this action would minimize the potential confusion and idiosyncratic interpretations of what would be required to complete the task. She would begin this process by explaining the section of the team's charter that listed the task, the criteria that would be applied to determining the team's effectiveness in relation to achieving this task, and the parameters that must be adhered to when completing task-related activities. Ellen would follow this explanation with an activity designed to get team members to process their understanding of the task by putting it into their own words.

NORMS AND ROLES

Experience had taught Ellen that each member would bring to the team a certain set of assumptions about the types of behavior that would be appropriate. Experience had also taught her that these assumptions would rarely, if ever, be discussed explicitly by the members, which would result in the development of norms that were ineffective for completion of the assigned task. Ellen remembered her experiences serving on the school district's Curriculum Council. Even though the assistant superintendent had lacked experience as an elementary school teacher, the council members had deferred to his opinion. The elementary-level members of the council had had the knowledge and expertise necessary to inform the decisions, but their input had been valued less than the assistant superintendent's because of his position in the organization. Although this weighting of input may have preserved the hierarchical structure of the organization, it had not lead the group to make the highest-quality decisions.

To promote norms that would lead to effective group functioning, Ellen decided that she would focus explicit attention on the types of behavior that would be valued and the ways in which team members' work toward task completion would be managed. She knew that even though she would begin to do this at the start-up meeting, the established norms would evolve over the life span of the team. However, by providing assistance in the beginning phase of the team's work, Ellen would help get this ongoing process off to a good start.

Similarly, Ellen realized that all groups function more effectively when the members know each other's responsibilities. In her experience, group members often found it reassuring and productive to know who was assuming what role in the group. Furthermore, knowing the responsibilities for each assigned role was valuable because it helped prevent overlap in the completion of work or incompletion of important tasks. With this in mind, Ellen decided on the team's various roles and responsibilities.

Sample Prereferral Intervention Team Roles and Responsibilities

- *Team coordinator:* This person has the responsibility and authority to coordinate team activities. He or she receives case referrals, establishes case priorities, schedules team meetings, and consults with referring teachers. He or she also locates, assigns, and arranges for qualified individuals to provide direct consultation to the referring teacher.
- *Resource group:* This group consists of all members of the prereferral intervention team with the exception of the referring teacher. These professionals are responsible for using their experience and expertise to generate alternatives for the referring teacher. If they have training in the agreed-upon assessment and intervention strategies, they may be assigned to provide direct consultation to the referring teacher.
- *Consultant:* This person has been trained in or has experience with implementing the agreed-upon assessment and intervention strategies. At a minimum, he or she demonstrates the technique and provides follow-up assistance. This person may or may not be a member of the prereferral intervention team.
- *Referring teacher:* This is the person who has attempted a number of interventions to address a student challenge and is now actively seeking new ideas. He or she selects the ideas to be implemented as interventions and actively participates in the direct consultation process.

Ellen needed to decide which team member would serve as the team coordinator. She wanted someone who was committed to the prereferral intervention team concept, was willing and able to coordinate team efforts, possessed demonstrated ability for following up on group decisions, and had the knowledge and skills required for facilitating groups. After a careful review of the members she had selected to serve on the team, Ellen chose Donna Walters. Based on what Ellen knew of Donna's performance as a guidance counselor, she met the criteria established for a team coordinator.

THE START-UP MEETING

Now that Ellen knew what she wanted to accomplish in her initial meeting with the prereferral intervention team, she sat down to develop the meeting agenda (Figure 4.1). Ellen communicated this agenda to team members, arranged substitute teachers for those members who required them, and obtained all of the necessary supplies and materials for the meeting.

Figure 4.1   Sample Prereferral Intervention Team Start-Up Meeting Agenda

---

Date:	**9/27/06**
Time:	**1:00–3:15 p.m.**
Location:	**principal's conference room**

Agenda Items

- Introductions/ice-breaker
- Review of team charter
  - o Who are the core members of the prereferral intervention team?
  - o What are the team's tasks?
  - o How will the team's effectiveness in meeting these tasks be evaluated?
  - o What are the parameters that the team must work within when completing the tasks?
  - o What are the resources available to the team, and how can they be accessed?

- Task redefinition activity
- Team norms activity
- Team roles and responsibilities
- Date for initial team training on collaborative problem-solving process
- Questions, comments, concerns

On the day of the start-up meeting, team members gathered in the principal's conference room. After a few minutes spent socializing, Ellen brought the meeting to order. She began with a brief review of the meeting agenda, after which she facilitated a brief ice-breaker designed to help team members get acquainted with one another and to establish a positive emotional climate. Next, she distributed a copy of the team charter to each member. The next 20 minutes were spent reviewing this charter in an effort to answer the questions on the meeting agenda. It was now time to conduct the task redefinition activity.

Ellen directed the team members to put away the team charter and then provided them with individual writing time to complete this statement: "The task for the school's prereferral intervention team is. . . ." After approximately two minutes, each team member was paired with a partner to share their responses. Ellen directed the partners to write down the ideas that they had in common or agreed on. Next, sets of partners combined to make foursomes, and the process was repeated. Then each group response was shared aloud. Ellen noted and then discussed with the group the discrepancies being shared. After a whole-group discussion, the team came to an agreement about what the task was and what it required. (Resource B #2 is a more detailed example of this task activity.)

The next activity that Ellen led the team through was the development of positive group norms. (This activity can be found in more detail in Resource B #3.) Using a team as an example, Ellen introduced the idea of effective behavioral norms. She stated, "We have all been part of a team. In any team there are certain rules or expectations for what we could or couldn't do and how we should behave. What were some of the rules or expectations on teams you have been a part of?" She facilitated the sharing of responses. After several minutes of listening to responses, she stated, "Most of what has been suggested are behaviors that have helped the team work successfully as a group. Just like these teams, our prereferral intervention team must have agreements or expectations for the group to function effectively." Next she asked, "What are some of the behaviors, both positive and negative, that you have experienced as a member of a team?" As team members offered answers, she recorded them on a T-chart.

Sample Responses to Group Norms Activity

Positive Team Behaviors	Negative Team Behaviors
Be on time.	Engage in side conversation.
Come prepared.	Dominate the discussion.
Focus on the task.	Do other work.
Share ideas and opinions.	Criticize people, not ideas.
Offer support and acceptance.	
Have fun.	

After listing the positive and negative team behaviors, Ellen initiated and then facilitated a discussion focused on the messages that these behaviors sent to members of a team. Now that the group appeared to understand the value of having a set of basic agreements, Ellen provided a starter list of possible agreements. She added more suggestions until the group concluded that all possibilities had been exhausted.

The initial list included too many agreements to be realistic. To prioritize the list so that it reflected only the most important agreements, Ellen led the team in an activity. She began by having team members divide a piece of paper into three equal columns. Next, she informed them that they each had 100 points and could "spend" them among each of the sample agreements listed. As points were spent on one agreement, they were subtracted from the total of 100. After having team members complete the task individually, Ellen directed them to share there scores with a group of three to four other members. As she listened to the group discussions, she realized that they helped team members clarify their thinking about the agreements. She was surprised by how poignant the members' explanations were as they shared why they valued one agreement over another.

Upon concluding this small-group sharing, Ellen informed the team members that they could now redistribute their personal points if any of their priorities had changed as a result of their small-group discussions. Then she collected all of the sheets and tallied the number of points spent on each item. The result of this tally was the group's final agreements.

Sample Final Agreements for Team Norms Activity

- We will start and end our meetings on time.
- We will actively listen to each other's ideas and opinions.
- We will place value on opinions based on the knowledge and skills of the individual and not the position that person holds.
- We will remain focused on the topic or task.
- We will come to meetings prepared.

To conclude this first meeting, Ellen reviewed team members' roles and the corresponding responsibilities associated with each role. Next, she informed them of the date, time, and location for the training they would receive on the collaborative problem-solving process. After answering the team members' questions, Ellen thanked them for their participation in this session and brought the meeting to a close.

THE IMPORTANCE OF THE START-UP MEETING

Research findings leave little room for doubt about the long-term effects of what happens at team start-up (Hackman, 1990). Groups that get off to a good start tend to perform better over time, whereas the problems of those that struggle in the beginning tend to compound as time goes on. Thus, it is critical for prereferral intervention teams to achieve success in the early phase of their work together.

Research findings also demonstrate that the best time for authoritative intervention is at the beginning of a group's life (Hackman, 1990). The behaviors of the educational leader are potent at this time. To launch a prereferral intervention team onto a productive path, the educational leader must facilitate the team's accomplishment of several tasks.

Critical Tasks to Be Accomplished at the Start-Up Meeting

- Ensure that team members accurately understand who is and is not a core member of the team.
- Ensure that team members accurately understand the assigned task, the effectiveness criteria, the task parameters, and the resources available.
- Ensure that the team develops initial positive behavioral norms and that roles and responsibilities are clearly understood.

INITIAL PREREFERRAL INTERVENTION TEAM TRAINING

As an educational leader, it will be one of your goals to have team members obtain expertise in collaborative problem-solving strategies. To achieve this, you must provide high-quality professional development. There are two basic rules to follow when preparing to train teachers in collaborative problem solving. First, the training must be done in teams. According to Moreland, Argote, and Krishnan (1998), training team members together rather than as separate individuals can jump-start the development of performance-enhancing team processes. A team whose members learn how to work together, and then stay together to further build their collective competencies, is almost certain to develop into a more effective team than would otherwise be the case. Second, training should occur prior to the team working with its "clients." What follows is a description of Ellen's efforts to provide this initial training.

The prereferral intervention team members gathered in the principal's conference room. After enjoying a continental breakfast and some informal socializing, they took their seats. Ellen distributed the handouts and then reviewed the agenda (Figure 4.2) and objectives for this training session.

Ellen then projected an overhead showing a flowchart of the prereferral intervention process (Figure 4.3). She proceeded to go through the steps in this flowchart in order to provide team members with a global view of the collaborative problem-solving process from beginning to end. Next, Ellen shared with the team members the basic form they would be using to structure and document their actions (Figure 4.4). In addition to describing the

Figure 4.2   Sample Prereferral Intervention Team Training Agenda

Date:	**10/3/06**
Time:	**9:15–11:45 a.m.**
Location:	**principal's conference room**

Agenda Items

- Overview of the prereferral intervention process
- Explanation of the Prereferral Intervention Plan components
- Explanation of the four steps in the collaborative problem-solving process
  - problem identification
  - problem analysis
  - plan implementation
  - plan review

- Role-play activity
- Questions, comments, and concerns

information required in each section. she linked each step in the flowchart with a section of the Prereferral Intervention Plan.

Ellen answered any questions that the team members had and then gave them a short break. After approximately 10 minutes. they reconvened and Ellen focused their attention on an overhead transparency (Figure 4.5).

Ellen proceeded to supplement this visual with an expanded description of the problem identification process:

The prereferral intervention team process begins with the teacher defining the problem in observable terms. He or she must also obtain a reliable baseline estimate of the frequency, intensity, and/or duration of the behavior of concern. I will be conducting a separate training for the remainder of the staff on how to complete these steps. After identifying the problem and collecting the required baseline data, the referring teacher will complete sections I and II of the prereferral intervention form. He or she will place the form in a sealed envelope and then put it in the team coordinator's mailbox.

At or very near the same time. the teacher will also notify the parents about his or her concern and the fact that the

Figure 4.3   Prereferral Intervention Process (also found in Resource B #4)

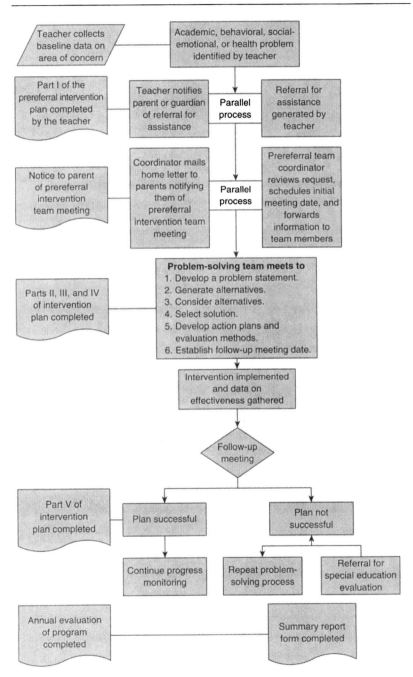

Figure 4.4 Prereferral Intervention Plan (also found in Resource B #5)

I. Referral Documentation

Student's name: _____ Grade: _____Teacher: _____
Student's address: _____ Phone number: _____
Gender: _____ Ethnicity: _____ English language proficiency: _____
Free or reduced lunch ☐
Referral date: _____
Parent has been notified of this referral ☐
Primary reason for referral (check only one)
☐ Academic concern   ☐ Behavior concern
☐ Social concern   ☐ Health concern
☐ Other

II. Referral (All statements must be in observable, measurable terms)

Student performance desired in the classroom: _____
Current student performance (baseline data): _____

Interventions attempted	Results

Other relevant information the team should consider: _____

III. Problem Analysis

Date and time of initial problem-solving meeting: _____
Meeting participants: _____
Problem statement: _____
Generation of alternatives:

Option	Advantages	Disadvantages

Teacher-selected alternative(s): _____

IV. Intervention Plan

Objective: By _____, _____ will demonstrate the ability to _____, as measured by _____.

Strategies to be implemented:

Strategy	Person responsible	When

Consultant: _____

Method(s) for collecting data and monitoring progress: _____

Date and time of initial follow-up meeting: _____

V. Plan Review

Date and time of meeting: _____

Meeting participants: _____

Identified concern	Baseline performance	Postintervention

Next Steps

☐ Plan successful; continue monitoring progress.

☐ Plan not successful; repeat problem-solving process.

☐ Plan not successful; refer for special education evaluation.

referral process has been initiated. The teacher will tell the parents that a meeting will be scheduled and they should expect to hear from the prereferral intervention team coordinator. The coordinator will review the form and then establish the initial meeting date and time. The date and time will be communicated to the appropriate team members, and a copy of the referral from will be disseminated. Team members will review the form and begin to

Figure 4.5   Overhead Transparency: Step 1 (also found in Resource B #6)

Step 1: Problem Identification

- Teacher
  - defines problem
  - requests assistance
  - notifies parent
  - submits referral form
- Team Coordinator
  - reviews form
  - schedules initial team meeting
  - notifies team members

think about possible solutions to the presenting problem. Let us now turn to the second step, problem analysis.

Ellen proceeded to use another overhead transparency (Figure 4.6) to explain the next step in the prereferral intervention process: problem analysis. In her explanation, Ellen provided the following information:

Usually, no mechanism exists for a reinterpretation of the teacher's initial perception of the situation, even though such early perceptions may not represent an accurate reflection of

Figure 4.6   Overhead Transparency: Step 2 (also found in Resource B #7)

Step 2: Problem Analysis

- Resource Group
  - validates problem statement
  - identifies variables contributing to the problem
  - generates ideas and solutions
- Referring Teacher
  - chooses strategy to implement
- Team Coordinator
  - facilitates completion of documentation
  - facilitates identification of consultant
  - schedules initial follow-up meeting

the actual problem. Therefore, the first thing the team will do is validate the accuracy of the problem statement. In the handout [Figure 4.7], you will find questions that can be used to clarify the problem statement provided by the teacher.

Figure 4.7   Problem Statement Validation Questions (also found in Resource B #8)

- Can you give a specific example of what you mean by _____?
- In your class, what would we actually see that would mean _____ to you?
- What specific task is this student having difficulty completing?
- What response is expected of the student that he or she is not providing currently?
- Is the concern one of the quantity produced or of the quality of the product?
- If we were in your class observing this student, what would we see in relation to the problem you have identified?
- Do you see this problem primarily resulting from a lack of skill, knowledge, motivation, or something else?
- How does this student's problem compare with the functioning of other students in your class?

When validating the problem statement, it is important to make sure that this is not communicated as an interrogation, but rather is conducted as an activity to make sure that everyone understands the nature of the problem presented. After making sure that the problem statement is an accurate reflection of the teacher's concern, the team will move on to identifying the instructional and student variables that may be contributing to the problem. The next handout (Figure 4.8), lists questions that can be used to identify the variables that may be contributing to the problem.

With these variables identified, the resource group will generate alternative ideas and solutions to address the identified problem. These ideas and solutions will be listed so that they can be referred to later. After the brainstorming has been completed, the referring teacher will analyze and choose among the ideas developed by the resource team. This solution may even be a combination of the ideas presented. The key is that the referring teacher must retain ownership over the final selection of the solution. With the solution selected, the team will determine the objective to be met, the criterion for success, the strategies to be implemented, the roles and responsibilities of the implementers, the time period for implementation, methods for collecting data and

Figure 4.8   Problem Analysis Questions (also found in Resource B #9)

Behavioral

- In what other settings or classes does this behavior occur?
- If it doesn't occur in other settings, what accounts for the difference?
- What happens just before the behavior occurs?
- What happens just after the behavior occurs?

Academic

- How do you give directions for completing the task?
- How does the student receive the information (e.g., orally, visually)?
- How is the student expected to respond (e.g., writing, reading, spoken)?
- How much practice is provided for completing this type of task?
- What kind of feedback do you give the student? How often?
- How does the student perform when assisted?
- What type of assistance works?

General

- What does the student do well?
- What are times when things are better?
- What is different about those times when things are better?

---

monitoring progress, and procedures for evaluating intervention effectiveness. One role that must be assigned at this point is that of the consultant. The next handout (Figure 4.9) describes the role of the consultant.

Often, the prereferral intervention team develops high-quality intervention plans for the referring teacher to implement. Unfortunately, the referring teacher frequently is not provided with the necessary knowledge, skills, or support to ensure proper implementation of the proposed interventions. Ironically, if the referring teacher already had the knowledge and skills, and viewed the intervention as likely to produce the desired outcomes, then the intervention would most likely already have been implemented as intended. Thus, there is frequently a gap between intended interventions and the teacher's ability to implement them, which results in the interventions being done differently than they were originally designed.

To improve this situation, the team should use a direct consultation model. First, the team will identify the consultant. To serve

Figure 4.9   Consultant's Role (also found in Resource B #10)

- The consultant is an individual trained in and experienced with implementing the recommended assessment and intervention strategies. He or she may or may not be a member of the prereferral intervention team.
- The consultant's objective is to ensure that the referring teacher has the knowledge and skills necessary for implementing the agreed-upon intervention strategies.
- At a minimum, the consulting process shall include the following:
  o providing any relevant literature to the referring teacher to read prior to conducting the in-class demonstration
  o conducting an in-class demonstration for the referring teacher to observe
  o observing and coaching the referring teacher in the implementation of the process
  o providing ongoing opportunities for the referring teacher to ask questions and seek feedback on implementation efforts

as a consultant, an individual must have training and experience with successful implementation of the recommended assessment and intervention strategies. A consultant may be any member of the school staff or, whenever possible, the school district.

Next, the consultant will provide the referring teacher with any relevant literature related to the assessment or intervention strategy. The teacher is to read this literature prior to the consultant performing an in-class demonstration of the strategies. After doing so, the teacher will observe the consultant's in-class demonstration of the strategies. Soon after the observation, the consultant and the teacher will meet to discuss the observation, which is when the teacher will have the opportunity to ask questions and seek clarification on what was observed. Near the end of this meeting, the consultant and the teacher will arrange a time for the consultant to observe the teacher as he or she implements the strategies. After observing the teacher's implementation of the strategies, the consultant will provide feedback and coaching. At this point, they will decide whether continued assistance is necessary.

At this point in the process, the team should have completed sections III and IV of the prereferral intervention team plan. Before concluding the meeting and moving on to plan implementation, the team will schedule the initial follow-up meeting. Figure 4.10 explains Step 3: plan implementation.

Figure 4.10   Overhead Transparency: Step 3 (also found in
                  Resource B #11)

Step 3: Plan Implementation

- Referring Teacher
  - ○ implements plan
  - ○ monitors implementation results
  - ○ seeks assistance from team coordinator and consultant as necessary

- Team Coordinator
  - ○ meets with referring teacher and, when appropriate, the consultant
  - ○ serves as link to resource team

With regard to this transparency, Ellen simply stated the following:

Regardless of the quality of the plan, the team develops implementation, but the referring teacher remains the most crucial
step in the process. The referring teacher must systematically
monitor the implementation results by collecting and organizing data. Doing this will increase the objectivity of the
judgments made regarding the efficacy of the intervention.
The team coordinator will meet with the teacher and, when
appropriate, the consultant to check on progress and will
serve as the link between the referring teacher, the consultant, and any additional resources or support needed during
the implementation process.

Ellen provided an explanation of the final step in the prereferral intervention process using the transparency shown in Figure
4.11. She briefly explained this final step:

Figure 4.11   Overhead Transparency: Step 4 (also found in
                  Resource B #12)

Step 4: Plan Review

- Teacher and Prereferral Intervention Team
  - ○ compare student's pre- and postintervention performance
  - ○ decide on next steps

The final step in the prereferral intervention process is the plan review. At this follow-up meeting, the referring teacher and the prereferral intervention team evaluate the effectiveness of the interventions implemented. This is done through a direct comparison of the student's postintervention performance and the original baseline data. If the plan has proven effective, then the team's involvement ceases. If the plan has not proven effective, then the team determines the next steps to be taken (i.e., revision of the original plan or referral for a special education evaluation).

Next, Ellen explained to the team that they would be conducting a role-play. In preparation, she distributed and then reviewed the student information in Figure 4.12.

After allowing the team members time to read the information and ask clarifying questions, Ellen assigned roles for the role-play activity. One member assumed the role of the referring teacher, Ellen assumed the role of the parent, and the rest of the members served as either the team coordinator or the resource group. After completing the problem analysis step, the team members reflected on their performance. First, Ellen asked them to describe what they had done well and what they could improve on for the next time. After the team members finished providing feedback, Ellen offered her observations and constructive suggestions.

For the next activity, Ellen assumed the role of the teacher. She brought back the intervention plan that had been developed in the previous role-play. Even though it was fictitious, Ellen provided postintervention data to compare with the preintervention data. Playing their roles, the team members reviewed the data and decided on the appropriate next step. As in the previous role-play, they reflected on their performance and identified areas for future improvement.

Having completed these activities with the team, Ellen accomplished the critical objectives for the initial training of her school's prereferral intervention team:

Critical Tasks to Be Accomplished in the Initial Team Training

- Ensure that team members understand the flow of the process from the point of referral to the plan review and determination of next steps.

(Continued)

Figure 4.12 Sample Prereferral Intervention Team Plan Referral

---

I. Referral Documentation

Student's name: Jake Green   Grade: 3   Teacher: Mrs. X
Student's address: 113 Blackwell Lane   Phone number: 973-008-0090
Gender: M   Ethnicity: White   English language proficiency: Proficient
Free or reduced lunch: No
Referral date: 10/11/06
Parent has been notified of this referral: Yes
Primary reason for referral (check only one)

- ☐ **Academic concern**   ☑ **Behavior concern**
- ☐ **Social concern**   ☐ **Health concern**
- ☐ **Other**

II. Referral (All statements must be in observable, measurable terms)

Student performance desired in the classroom: Jake will accept constructive criticism from his teacher by using the corrective feedback provided to improve his performance.

Current student performance (baseline data): Jake received teacher-provided constructive criticism 11 times between 9/27/06 and 10/9/06. In response to the constructive criticism provided, Jake made inappropriate verbal responses three times, cried seven times, and threw something once. There were no incidents in which one of these behavioral responses did not occur.

Interventions attempted	Results
Teacher provided frequent positive feedback.	Jake accepted positive feedback but still could not accept constructive criticism.
Teacher attempted to speak privately with Jake about behavior.	Jake denied that any problem existed.
Teacher provided Jake with a time-out in response to his inappropriate verbal responses and throwing of class materials.	Jake appeared remorseful after each incident and apologized for his behaviors.

Other relevant information the team should consider: According to his mother, Jake has never demonstrated this type of behavior before. He does not display these behaviors at home and has no history of this type of behavior in school. He has demonstrated difficulty adjusting to the demands of the work this year and has especially struggled in mathematics.

(Continued)

- Ensure that team members understand the requirements of each section of the intervention plan as well as how the parts of the plan are linked to the steps in the prereferral intervention process.
- Ensure that team members complete the actions required in the problem analysis and plan review steps.

In sum, although Ellen knew there remained substantial room for growth, she was confident that the team members had the initial skills and knowledge required to complete their tasks.

STAFF AWARENESS

The success of the prereferral intervention process partially depends on how and when it is used by the school faculty. To use the process effectively, staff members must know the purpose of the team, their responsibilities as the referring teacher, and the process for requesting assistance. The educational leader should provide information on these topics to the staff after he or she has completed the steps in the start-up phase. This can be done by way of a staff meeting, a memo, or a combination of both. In addition, it is valuable to place this information in a staff handbook so that staff members can refer to it as needed. The following is a sample describing the type of information that the handbook may convey:

Sample Staff Handbook Explanation

The purpose of the school's prereferral intervention team is to engage in collegial, collaborative problem-solving activities focused on assisting teachers in developing strategies for challenging student behavior or academic or health concerns. This is a voluntary activity and is not intended to serve as a barrier to initiating referrals for special education evaluations. Any teacher initiating a referral to this team is expected to complete Parts I and II of the Prereferral Intervention Plan form. Copies of this form are located in _____. Upon completing this form,

(Continued)

(Continued)

submit it in a sealed envelope to _____. He or she will then contact you to inform you of the status of your request and, if appropriate, schedule the initial prereferral intervention team meeting. All discussion of information pertaining to the intervention process must be held in strict confidence. Staff members are not to discuss any personally identifiable information with anyone outside the official function of this process. Should you have any questions about completing this form or the purpose of this team, please contact _____.

STAFF TRAINING

A critical part of an effective prereferral intervention program is the use of data for effective decision making. One critical element of data collection and use is the establishment of a baseline data set, which will provide valuable information to the team about the nature of the problem. Without baseline data, the team will not have an accurate perception of the intensity or severity of the concern. This data will also be critical for determining the degree of effectiveness for the interventions applied. If there is no baseline data set, it is very difficult to determine whether an intervention led to improvement.

The referring teacher must establish a baseline data set. It has been my experience that most teachers do not know how to complete this task because they have not been trained in curriculum-based measurement strategies as part of their pre- or in-service training. Keeping this in mind, the following is a sequence of basic steps that teachers should use for establishing a baseline data set. Although the example deals with basic reading skills, the same process can be used for any observable, measurable student behavior.

Rhonda is a kindergarten teacher with concerns about Tara's lack of fluency and accuracy in naming the letters of the alphabet. The curriculum goal for Rhonda's school states that kindergarteners should be able to accurately name 26 randomly placed letters in a one-minute time period by the end of January. After approximately eight weeks of school, it appears that Tara is not making progress toward this goal, and she is falling significantly behind her classmates in this curricular area.

Figure 4.13 Example Reading Graph

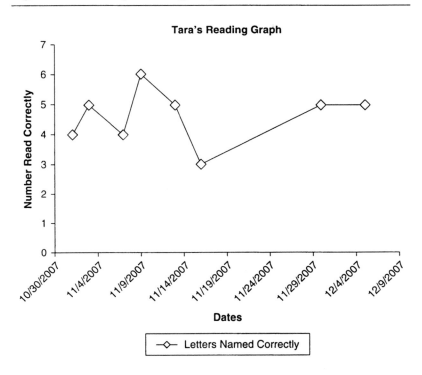

To test her assumption, Rhonda develops a series of one-minute tests in which Tara is asked to name randomly placed letters. Rhonda repeats this activity twice a week for four weeks. Using a software program developed by Effective Leadership Solutions, Rhonda graphs these eight data points (Figure 4.13).

Rhonda brings this data and graph to a prereferral intervention team meeting. At the meeting, the team reviews this data and develops an intervention plan, the goal of which is for Tara to meet the curriculum goal of accurately reading 26 letters per minute by the end of January. To measure the results of the interventions developed by the team, Rhonda is to continue assessing Tara's ability to accurately identify random letters. More specifically, Rhonda will continue to conduct one-minute assessments two times per week. The team uses the long-range goal data point and the median plotted baseline data point to determine an aim line (Figure 4.14). This line is a graphical representation of the average rate of Tara's expected progress if she is to meet the goal by the date established.

Figure 4.14   Aim Line Graph

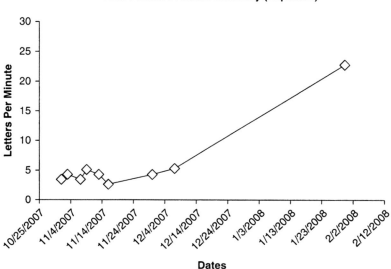

The team also decides to reconvene before the next scheduled meeting date at the end of January if Tara demonstrates no progress for three consecutive assessments or if she does not demonstrate an average of two additional letters per minute for two consecutive weeks. Rhonda continues to graph the results and eventually brings additional data back to the prereferral intervention team (Figure 4.15).

After reviewing this data, the team concludes that the intervention was successful. Tara has met the established goal based on the assessment data collected and graphed by Rhonda. They decide that Rhonda should continue monitoring Tara's progress but that the services of the team are no longer necessary for meeting Tara's academic needs.

This example is hypothetical, but it includes the critical steps that a teacher must follow in using data to establish a baseline, monitor progress, and determine the effectiveness of an intervention:

1. Determine a targeted behavior that is observable and measurable.

2. Collect data to establish a baseline through either brief performance assessments (academic) or recording of

Figure 4.15   Results Graph

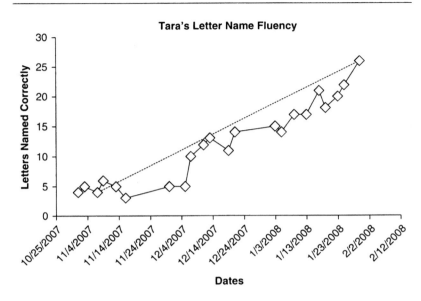

observational data (behavior). At least six to eight data points collected at different times are necessary to establish a baseline.

3. Determine the level of performance required for an intervention to be deemed effective. This is the long-range goal data point. Also determine the amount of time that will be provided to reach this goal.

4. Graph this data. Draw an aim line between the median plotted baseline data point and the long-range goal data point.

5. Determine the incremental progress that will be necessary for reaching the long-range goal data point. For example, if a student needs to read 24 more words per minute accurately in a six-week time period, the average weekly gain would need to be 4 additional words per minute, per week.

6. Establish a set of rules (such as the following) that will determine whether a student is making adequate progress toward the established goal. If the student is not

making adequate progress according to the established rule(s), the teacher should notify the prereferral intervention team coordinator. A meeting should then be held to review the intervention strategies.

Generic Decision Rules for Interventions

- If three consecutive data points are below the goal line, an intervention change should be made.
- If six consecutive data points are above the goal line, the goal is too low and needs to be revised upward.
- If neither applies, continue with the intervention and progress monitoring.

7. The teacher is to continue gathering and plotting data as agreed to in the prereferral intervention team meeting.

8. This data and the resulting graph are reviewed at the follow-up prereferral intervention team meeting. Next steps are determined based in part on the review of this data.

Monitoring student progress through the collection, plotting, and analysis of data is critical for the success of a prereferral intervention program. This data assists the referring teacher and members of the team in determining the nature of the behavior that is of concern. In addition, it makes it possible for the teacher and team members to monitor student progress toward the established goal. Using the data and the established decision rule(s), the referring teacher will request a timely meeting of the prereferral intervention team if a student is not making adequate progress. At this point, the team can review the data and interventions to determine whether the plan needs to be revised. Last, when the team reconvenes for the scheduled follow-up meeting, there will be data to consider when judging the effectiveness of the program and the next steps to be taken.

CONCLUSION

The third phase for an educational leader who is considering revising or implementing a prereferral intervention team is start-up. The steps of this phase are outlined in Figure 4.16.

Figure 4.16 Phase 3: Start-Up

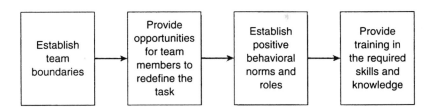

Within this phase, the educational leader must establish who is accountable for the outcomes of the team's work and, as a result, shares responsibility for the completion of the assigned tasks. Furthermore, the educational leader must review the team's task, which was refined in Phase 2, to make sure that it is clearly understood by the members of the team. The educational leader must facilitate the development of positive behavioral norms and then assign and communicate task-appropriate roles. This can be accomplished at a team start-up meeting. Shortly after this start-up meeting, the educational leader must provide team members with high-quality training designed to provide the initial knowledge and skills required for completion of the team's tasks. At a minimum, training should increase the members' understanding of the entire prereferral intervention process, familiarize them with the components and use of the required forms, and allow them to role-play with feedback on collaborative problem-solving skills. In addition, all staff members in the school must be made aware of the team's purpose and should be trained in the skills necessary for effectively participating in the process. The final phase, assistance, is the subject of Chapter 5.

CHAPTER FIVE

The Assistance Phase

A manager is an assistant to his men.

—Thomas J. Watson

Once the prereferral intervention team has been formed and established, it will, to a considerable extent, control its own future. Yet the educational leader can still assist the team by taking three actions:

- Eliminate (or at least minimize) barriers impeding completion of the group's task.
- Dedicate time for structured group reflection and learning.
- As necessary, assist the group with its work processes.

ELIMINATING BARRIERS

Ellen's experiences serving as a member of school teams had taught her that some of the features of the initial design are likely to be flawed. She had also learned that most of the time team members accept these flaws both as inevitable and as things that cannot be changed. As a result, they do not take the actions necessary for making changes to their context or structure. Ultimately, this lack of action leads to lower-quality products or decisions.

Ellen did not want this problem to occur with her school's prereferral intervention team. So she decided to provide scheduled, structured opportunities for explicit review and, if necessary, renegotiation of the team's design and context. The specific focus for these review sessions would be discussion of the aspects of the situation that impede the group's performance and what, if anything, could be done about them. Ellen was well aware of the temptation she would face to solve the group's problems herself. However, she knew that she had to resist this temptation if she was to succeed in getting the team members to take responsibility for managing their own affairs. Her role in these meetings would be to facilitate their efforts to identify and resolve factors limiting their ability to complete their assigned tasks. Ellen decided to schedule these review sessions monthly during the first marking period and then quarterly after that.

TECHNOLOGY

In various contexts, prereferral intervention team members and teachers attempting to use the team's services express frustration with the time required to complete the process and the necessary paperwork (Askamit & Rankin, 1993). To address this issue, educational leaders can use technology to help educators manage the process. Effective Leadership Solutions has developed a prereferral intervention software program called SPIRIT that is designed to automate the management of the forms and procedures provided in this book. Dropdown menus and templates enable the prereferral intervention team to create, share, save, and archive parental notices and prereferral intervention plans. In addition, all of the evaluation activities and reports described in Chapter 7 can be completed automatically through the features of this program. It is a user-friendly tool for improving the efficiency and effectiveness of your school's prereferral intervention team. (For more information on this program, visit effectiveleadershipsolutions.com.)

REFLECTION ACTIVITIES

Ellen had been a part of various school teams in which group functioning was never thoughtfully or systematically examined. She always felt that despite the fact that learning how to function together effectively is essential to the success of teams, it is frequently pushed aside in favor of emphasis on task completion. As a result, teams and their members rarely improve their ability to work effectively or efficiently on future tasks. Frequently, team members pay so much attention to the task they are doing that they neglect to examine the processes they are using. Ellen's goal was to achieve a balance between task completion and reflection on group processes. Because of the tendency to emphasize task completion, she knew that group reflection was not likely to occur unless she scheduled time for the activities. She decided that the examination of barriers impeding the team's performance could be combined with reflection activities. With that decision made, Ellen provided the dates of the review sessions to the prereferral intervention team coordinator to place on the team's calendar. These meetings would be referred to on the calendar as "team maintenance" meetings.

It would be relatively easy to discuss barriers impeding the group's performance. Ellen would ask what was interfering with successful completion of the team's activities and have a discussion based on the answers received. But how should the reflection activities be structured? After thinking about this for a while, Ellen concluded that she already had the criteria required for completing reflection activities. She would take the behavioral norms and roles developed earlier and turn them into a reflection form. The Prereferral Intervention Team Reflection Form (Figure 5.1) is the result of her efforts.

At each of the scheduled team maintenance meetings, each team member would individually complete this form. They would then compare and discuss their answers. This comparison and discussion would lead to the development of a collective goal statement to be revisited in the next team maintenance meeting. At that point, an evaluation would be made on progress toward attainment of the goal and either development of a new goal or revision of the existing one.

ASSISTANCE WITH GROUP PROCESSES

Ellen knew all too well that relationships among members of school teams often left much to be desired. She had experienced

Figure 5.1   Prereferral Intervention Team Reflection Form (also found in Resource B #13)

Directions: For each of the items below, please circle the response that indicates your level of agreement with the statement.

1 = strongly disagree   **2 = disagree**   **3 = agree**   **4 = strongly agree**

1. We start our meetings on time.	1	2	3	4
2. We end our meetings on time.	1	2	3	4
3. We actively listen to each other's ideas and opinions.	1	2	3	4
4. We weight the opinions of team members based on their knowledge and skill.	1	2	3	4
5. During meetings we remain focused on the topic or task.	1	2	3	4
6. We come to meetings having done the necessary preparations for completing the task.	1	2	3	4

Please Write a Brief Comment for Each of the Following Statements:

One thing that our team is doing well, which we want to continue, is:

One thing that our team could do better to function more effectively and efficiently would be:

Collective Goal Statement (to be completed by team)

Our collective goal is:

To achieve this goal we will:

We know we will have achieved this goal when:

---

situations in which team members experienced interpersonal competition and conflict. As a result, when a difficult or anxiety-arousing issue arose, they did not provide support to one another. Other times Ellen had served on teams that had been so oriented toward sharing support and positive feelings that the task itself was forgotten or neglected. Thus, she believed that enhancing the quality and balance of interpersonal processes among members of the prereferral intervention team was essential for improving the group's overall effectiveness. Ellen decided to focus her efforts on two specific aspects of the group process:

- coordinating team member's efforts and fostering their commitment
- helping team members weight individual inputs and share knowledge

Ellen had already determined that although it was not the most important aspect of the group process for prereferral intervention teams, effort would be a factor in determining the team's effectiveness. She reasoned that, as with all teams, the prereferral intervention team would function more effectively if members coordinated their activities in a manner that minimized the amount of effort wasted. She knew that although it was inevitable that there would be some difficulties in how well members coordinated their activities, she would remain sensitive to signs of difficulty in this area. If necessary, she would provide guidance to the team on ways that they could minimize wasted effort and improve member coordination. Her overarching goal in this area was to ensure that the team received the greatest possible contributions from its members.

Ellen believed that a second aspect impacting the effort applied to the task would be the team members' level of commitment to the group. If they valued their membership in the group and found working collaboratively to be rewarding, the overall level of effort put forth by the team members would increase considerably. Ellen believed that the importance of the task combined with positive behavioral norms would lead to high levels of commitment to the team.

More important to the success of this prereferral intervention team would be the level of knowledge and skill that team members brought to bear on the task. However, the value of this knowledge and skill might be limited by the weighting of team members' contributions. On multiple occasions, Ellen had witnessed educators turning to a supervisor when help or information was required. It was her opinion that educators as a group tended to be neither skilled nor practiced at sharing task-relevant knowledge with each other. She had often been part of a group in which the input of certain members was given extra credence for reasons that had little or nothing to do with their task-relevant knowledge or expertise. Sometimes the individual had more experience in education, had important or powerful political connections, or simply presented his or her views to the group especially persuasively. Ultimately, this led to a product or decision of lower quality than could have been achieved if the input had been considered based on task-relevant knowledge or expertise.

Ellen decided that one of her roles would be to monitor and facilitate how team members assessed and weighted one another's contributions to the work of the team. One method for doing this would be to use the reflection form she had designed. She also felt that, if necessary, she would directly intervene to make sure that members were weighting one another's contributions effectively. Although this ran the risk of "meddling" in the affairs of the team, she believed that it was critical to the overall success of the team. Regardless of how it was accomplished, Ellen knew that over time she would train the team members (and staff) to appropriately share with one another their task-relevant skills and knowledge.

CONCLUSION

The role of the educational leader does not end when the prereferral intervention team begins its task-completion activities. Instead, the educational leader must begin providing the team with assistance. The key aspects of this assistance are highlighted in Figure 5.2.

The educational leader must provide structured opportunities for team members to identify and, if possible, eliminate barriers that impede their ability to complete the assigned task. The educational leader must then schedule and facilitate reflection on the processes being used to complete tasks and make decisions. This is essential for the continuous improvement of team members' group process skills. Last, the educational leader must also provide process assistance to the team as required. Achievement of effective group functioning requires more than a

Figure 5.2 Phase 4: Providing Assistance

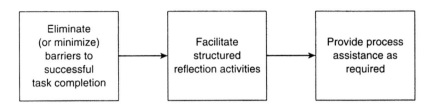

group of individuals, each of whom is well trained in a specific discipline. Skills for working in a group and utilizing group resources, such as being able to consider and synthesize divergent perspectives, are also necessary. Technology can be a valuable tool for managing and evaluating the prereferral intervention team process. Evaluating and reporting on the work of prereferral intervention teams is the subject of Chapter 6.

CHAPTER SIX

Evaluating Prereferral Intervention Teams

Social improvement is attained more readily by a concern with the quality of results than with the purity of motives.

—Eric Hoffer

Evaluation of prereferral intervention teams is both complex and multidimensional. Most of the tasks that the team will be expected to perform do not have clearly defined right-or-wrong answers. Furthermore, the team does not have control over many of the variables that influence the outcomes achieved. The team can generate potentially effective solutions and support the teacher in implementing those solutions, but the quality of the implementation of those solutions and the context in which they occur remain largely beyond the team's control. Despite these challenges, the team must attempt to evaluate the outcomes achieved. Identification of areas of strength and concern is necessary for the continuous improvement of prereferral intervention teams.

The educational leader must be concerned about more than outcomes when assessing prereferral intervention teams. Teacher and team member satisfaction with the processes are also important.

What happens during the prereferral intervention process will substantially affect both teachers' and team members' willingness and ability to participate in this process in the future. If effective outcomes are achieved at the cost of teacher and team member frustration and disillusionment, the process will not sustain long-term results. Thus, to assess the effectiveness of a collaborative teaching team, there must be analysis of both outcomes and personal and social criteria.

EVALUATION TOOLS

The first tool used to assess the effectiveness of the prereferral intervention process is the Prereferral Intervention Team Report (Figure 6.1). Completing this form will provide the team and other stakeholders with data on the number of requests for assistance, the nature of these requests, the characteristics of the students for which assistance has been requested, and the outcomes of the requests. The report can even be completed automatically by using the software described in Chapter 5. On a regularly scheduled basis (quarterly, semiannually, or annually), teams should complete and review the data contained in this report. How often the report should be completed is an administrative decision that depends on the needs of the school and the developmental level of the team.

The second tool used to evaluate prereferral intervention team activities is the Prereferral Intervention Team Rating Scale (Figure 6.2). Completing this scale takes approximately five minutes, and it provides data on the team members' perceptions of the processes used and overall satisfaction with serving as a member of the team. This form is intended to be completed by prereferral intervention team members on the same schedule as the Prereferral Intervention Team Report. However, depending on the nature of the situation or the needs of the team, it can be done more or less frequently. The information can be compiled and used to note areas of strength and areas in need of improvement.

To obtain a score from the Prereferral Intervention Team Rating Scale, follow these directions:

1. Make one copy of the tabulation worksheet shown in Figure 6.3.

Figure 6.1   Prereferral Intervention Team Report (also found in Resource B #14)

School: _____ Data organized by: _____ Date completed: _____

I. Total Number of Referrals: _____

II. Referrals by Grade Level

Grade level	Number of referrals	Percentage of total
K		
1		
2		
3		
4		
5		
6		
7		
8		
9		
10		
11		
12		

III. Referrals by Ethnicity

Ethnicity	Number of referrals	Percentage of total
White		
Black		
Hispanic/Latino		
Asian/Pacific Islander		
American Indian/Alaskan		

IV. Referrals by English Language Proficiency

Language proficiency	Number of referrals	Percentage of total
English only		
Limited English proficient		
Fluent English		

(Continued)

(Continued)

V. Referrals by Free or Reduced Lunch

Free or reduced lunch	Number of referrals	Percentage of total
Eligible		
Not eligible		

VI. Primary Reason for Referral

Characteristic	Academic		Behavior		Social		Health		Other	
	No.	%	No.	%	No.	%	No.	%	No.	%
K										
1										
2										
3										
4										
5										
6										
7										
8										
9										
10										
11										
12										
White										
Black										
Hispanic/Latino										
Asian/Pacific Islander										
American Indian/Alaskan										
English only										
Limited English proficient										
Fluent English										
Free or reduced lunch										

VII. Outcome of Referrals

Characteristic	Initial plan successful		Revised plan successful		Referral for evaluation	
	No.	%	No.	%	No.	%
K						
1						
2						
3						
4						
5						
6						
7						
8						
9						
10						
11						
12						
White						
Black						
Hispanic/Latino						
Asian/Pacific Islander						
American Indian/Alaskan						
English only						
Limited English proficient						
Fluent English						
Free or reduced lunch						

Figure 6.2   Prereferral Intervention Team Rating Scale (also found in Resource B #15)

Thank you for taking the time to complete this survey on our school's prereferral intervention team. Please answer *all* of the following statements by circling *one* of the five responses provided in the columns.

(A) Always   (M) Most of the time   (S) Some of the time   (R) Rarely   (N) Never

	A	M	S	R	N
1. The tasks to be achieved by the team were clear.	A	M	S	R	N
2. The tasks to be achieved by the team were motivating.	A	M	S	R	N
3. The team had the level of authority necessary for effectively completing the assigned tasks.	A	M	S	R	N
4. The composition of the team helped with the completion of the tasks.	A	M	S	R	N
5. The team had access to the information necessary for completing the tasks.	A	M	S	R	N
6. The team had access to the outside expertise necessary for completing the tasks.	A	M	S	R	N
7. Team members felt rewarded for completing the assigned tasks.	A	M	S	R	N
8. The team had the necessary material resources for completing the assigned tasks.	A	M	S	R	N
9. It was clearly understood who was a member of this team.	A	M	S	R	N
10. The norms and roles used by the team were helpful for completing the assigned tasks.	A	M	S	R	N
11. As a team, we had an opportunity to discuss with the school leadership any barriers that were impeding the group's performance.	A	M	S	R	N
12. As a team, we received assistance that helped us improve our group process.	A	M	S	R	N
13. As a team, we stopped periodically to reflect on and learn from our experiences.	A	M	S	R	N
14. I found the experience of serving on this team personally satisfying.	A	M	S	R	N
15. The experience of being on this team increased my skills in working as a member of a group.	A	M	S	R	N

2. Using each returned form, on the tabulation worksheet tally the number of people who selected a particular response. The scores translate as follows:

   (A) Always to a 4

   (M) Most of the time to a 3

   (S) Some of the time to a 2

   (R) Rarely to a 1

   (N) Never to a 0

3. Count the total number of people who responded to that question.

4. Multiply the number of 4s by 4, the number of 3s by 3, and so on.

5. Divide the sum by the total number of respondents.

6. Obtain an average score. Round the number obtained from the calculation to the nearest tenth. Place the score in the "Average" column on the same row of the tabulation worksheet. Repeat this step to obtain an average score for each question.

7. To obtain the overall effectiveness score, add all of the individual averages and write the total in the space labeled "Group Total."

8. Divide the group total by 15 (total number of questions) to obtain the total group rating score.

9. Use these scores to help determine areas of strength and areas in need of improvement:

   Less than 2.0 → In need of improvement

   2.1–2.5 → Marginal, may need to be improved

   2.6–3.4 → Average, no need for immediate improvement

   3.5–4.0 → An area of strength

For questions on which a low score was obtained, go back to the chapter of this book that addresses that aspect of prereferral intervention team performance. Review the information presented there, and determine what could be done differently to improve the performance of your school's team.

Figure 6.3   Prereferral Intervention Team Rating Scale Tabulation
Worksheet (also found in Resource B #16)

Question #	(A) – 4	(M) – 3	(S) – 2	(R) – 1	(N) – 0	Average
1						
2						
3						
4						
5						
6						
7						
8						
9						
10						
11						
12						
13						
14						
15						
	_____	/15 =	_____			
	Group		Group			
	Total		Rating			

The third tool used to evaluate the prereferral intervention process is the Teacher Satisfaction Survey (Figure 6.4). This tool provides data on the referring teacher's satisfaction with the assistance that he or she received. This form takes approximately five minutes to complete and should be completed by the referring teacher around the same time as the prereferral intervention team's plan review meeting. The results are likely to be more accurate if anonymity is provided to those responding.

Figure 6.4   Teacher Satisfaction Survey (also found in Resource B #17)

Recently you participated in a prereferral intervention team plan review meeting. This survey is designed to determine your level of satisfaction with the overall prereferral intervention process. Please answer *all* of the following statements by circling *one* of the five responses provided in the columns.

(SA) Strongly Agree   (A) Agree   (N) Neutral   (D) Disagree   (SD) Strongly Disagree

1. The amount of time required for completing the   SA   A   N   D   SD
   prereferral intervention process was reasonable.

2. The paperwork required for completing the   SA   A   N   D   SD
   prereferral intervention process was reasonable.

3. The intervention strategies developed as a   SA   A   N   D   SD
   result of the prereferral intervention process
   were things I did not think of on my own.

4. The intervention strategies developed as a result   SA   A   N   D   SD
   of the prereferral intervention process could be
   realistically implemented in my classroom.

5. I received the material resources needed for   SA   A   N   D   SD
   implementing the intervention strategies developed.

6. I received the emotional support required for   SA   A   N   D   SD
   implementing the intervention strategies developed.

7. I received training in the knowledge and skills   SA   A   N   D   SD
   necessary for implementing the interventions.

8. If confronted with a similar student concern in   SA   A   N   D   SD
   the future, I will feel more confident in my ability to
   independently solve the problem.

9. As a result of the prereferral intervention team   SA   A   N   D   SD
   experience, I have improved my skills for working
   with students who experience academic or
   behavioral problems.

10. I would recommend using the services of the   SA   A   N   D   SD
    prereferral intervention team to my colleagues.

Suggestions I have for improving the prereferral intervention process include:

Take the following steps to obtain a score from the Teacher Satisfaction Survey.

1. Make one copy of the tabulation worksheet shown in Figure 6.5.

2. Using each returned form, on the tabulation worksheet tally the number of people who selected a particular response. The scores for Questions 1 through 10 translate as follows:

   (SA) Strongly Agree to a 5

   (A) Agree to a 4

   (N) Neutral to a 3

   (D) Disagree to a 2

   (SD) Strongly Disagree to a 1

3. Count the total number of people who responded to that question.

4. Multiply the number of 5s by 5, the number of 4s by 4, and so on.

5. Divide the sum by the total number of respondents.

6. Obtain an average score. Round the number obtained from the calculation to the nearest tenth. Place the average score in the "Average" column on the same row of the tabulation worksheet. Repeat this step to obtain an average score for each question.

7. To obtain the overall teacher satisfaction survey score, add all of the individual averages and write the total in the space labeled "Group Total."

8. Divide the group total by 10 (total number of questions) to obtain the total group rating score.

9. Use these scores to help determine areas of strength and areas in need of improvement:

   Less than 2.5 → In need of improvement

   2.6–3.4 → Marginal, may need to be improved

   3.5–4.4 → Average, no need for immediate improvement

   4.5–5.0 → An area of strength

Figure 6.5   Teacher Satisfaction Survey Tabulation Worksheet (also found in Resource B #18)

Question #	(SA) – 5	(A) – 4	(N) – 3	(D) – 2	(SD) – 1	Average
1						
2						
3						
4						
5						
6						
7						
8						
9						
10						
	_____	/10 =	_____			
	Group		Group			
	Total		Rating			

If a trained outside observer wants to provide structured observational feedback to the team members regarding the fidelity with which they are implementing the model, that person can use the Prereferral Team Observation Form (Figure 6.6). To use this form, the observer must attend a team meeting and focus on determining the extent to which the desired behaviors occur.

DATA ANALYSIS AND ACTION PLANNING

Collecting and organizing data is a necessary but insufficient task. Once collected and organized, the educational leader must have a process for analyzing the data and using it to make the necessary program changes. It is preferable to complete this process collaboratively with members of the prereferral intervention team. Involvement in data analysis and action planning results in increased ownership for any resulting program changes. The

Figure 6.6   Prereferral Intervention Team Observation Form (also found in Resource B #19)

	Observed	Not Observed
Date:		
Observer:		
Baseline data for the student's area of concern was described in specific, measurable terms.		
The desired student replacement behavior was described in specific, observable terms.		
The team validated the accuracy of the teacher-provided problem statement.		
The team identified variables that potentially contributed to the student's behavior.		
The team brainstormed potential interventions to address the concern presented.		
The team identified potential advantages and disadvantages for each of the options brainstormed.		
The teacher selected an option(s) to implement as an intervention for addressing the student concern.		
The option(s) selected by the teacher has been translated into a specific, measurable goal statement.		
Responsibilities for carrying out the tasks for implementing the intervention(s) have been clearly identified.		
Methods and responsibilities for monitoring student progress have been clearly identified.		

Positive behaviors observed:

Recommendations/suggestions:

following is a sequence of actions that can be taken to analyze the data and plan for future program improvements:

1. Using the Priority-Setting Matrix shown in Figure 6.7, list the areas in need of improvement under the column "Area of Concern." This can be done on an overhead projector, a piece of chart paper, or individual copies of the matrix. Give each team member an appropriate amount of time to assign a value to the next three columns in the chart. Each item must be rated on a scale from 1 to 5, with 5 being the highest rating. The three columns relate to these questions:

   a. How much of an impact on achievement would a change in this area make?

   b. How much effort would it take to make significant changes regarding this issue?

   c. How feasible is it to make significant changes related to this issue?

2. Direct the team members to add the three ratings columns together and place the sum under the column "Total of Individual Ratings." The higher the total in this column, the more priority the item deserves.

3. Based on the individual rankings, each staff member chooses his or her top three priorities. The highest-priority item would receive a score of 5, the second-highest a 3, and the third-highest a 1.

4. Once participants have selected their top three priority areas, direct each team member to share his or her priorities and the score for each. After all of the areas have been shared, total the numbers.

5. The three highest-priority items from this activity will serve as the top priorities for action planning.

The Strategic Action Planning Form (Figure 6.8) should be used to create the plan for each item identified as in need of improvement. The first task for each of these items is to list all of the action steps that need to be taken. After completing all of the action steps, the educational leader must identify who will complete that step, when they will complete it by, and how you will know if the actions

Figure 6.7 Priority-Setting Matrix (also found in Resource B #20)

Area of Concern	Impact Rate each item 1–5, with 5 having the greatest impact.	Effort Rate each item 1–5, with 5 requiring the least amount of effort.	Feasibility Rate each item 1–5, with 5 being the most feasible.	Total of Individual Ratings	Individual Ranking Rank order three items only, with 5 as highest priority, 3 as second highest, and 1 as lowest.	Group Ranking

Figure 6.8   Strategic Action Planning Form (also found in Resource B #21)

Area in need of improvement	Action steps	Individual(s) responsible	Timeline	Evaluation

have been successful. Areas identified as in need of improvement must be examined to determine whether staff training or outside expertise is needed. If one or both of these are needed, it is the educational leader's responsibility to secure these educational resources. Revisiting these action plans will serve as a focal point of all subsequent data analysis and strategic planning sessions.

CONCLUSION

Properly used, data helps the educational leader and the prereferral intervention team assess and evaluate the effectiveness of the team's activities. Used judiciously and systematically, the collected data can be used to identify program strengths as well as areas in need of improvement. The process described in this chapter focuses prereferral intervention teams on continuous, incremental improvements toward desired outcomes.

CHAPTER SEVEN

Connecting Prereferral Intervention Teams and Response to Intervention

Implementing a response to intervention model is much like eating an elephant: If you try to do it all at once, you'll choke.

—John E. McCook

*R*esponse to intervention (RTI) gathered significant attention on December 3, 2004, when U.S. President George W. Bush signed the Individuals with Disabilities Educational Improvement Act. This reauthorized legislation included a section that prohibited state education agencies from requiring local education agencies to use a discrepancy model for identifying students with learning disabilities. Local education agencies were now given the choice to use either a discrepancy or an RTI model. If they choose to abandon the traditional discrepancy formula in favor of RTI, the decision would have implications for their current prereferral intervention programs.

Instead of abandoning prereferral intervention programs or attempting to operate both RTI and prereferral programs simultaneously, it makes sense to combine them. In fact, considering their complementary nature and their unique strengths, it may make sense to combine these programs regardless of the decision to abandon the discrepancy formula for identifying learning disabilities.

THE CONNECTION

One reason these programs can be combined is that they share many of the same goals and features. More specifically, both prereferral intervention programs and RTI models do the following:

- assign primary responsibility for implementation to general education personnel
- seek to provide support to at-risk students due to behavior and/or insufficient progress in academics
- require that the teachers implementing the interventions receive adequate levels of support and training
- require personnel to conduct ongoing monitoring of student progress in order to determine the effectiveness of the interventions attempted
- use collected data to determine the nature and intensity of interventions implemented
- require coordinated and flexible movement within the services offered by the school district
- require extensive and systematic communication between stakeholders and service providers

Due to these similarities, a school district operating both a prereferral intervention program and an RTI model would likely create a situation fraught with overlapping roles and responsibilities. At a minimum, these overlapping roles and responsibilities would result in confusion about who is responsible for what tasks. Yet choosing to operate only one or the other program would fail to capitalize on the strengths that are unique to each:

- RTI models employ universal screening procedures, which increases the probability that students will be appropriately identified.
- RTI models examine classroom results to determine whether any class has a disproportionate number of students falling within the bottom percentile. Doing this decreases the chances that instruction is the source of the problem.
- RTI models have a tiered structure that is linked to research-based instructional programs. Thus, interventions will be scientifically based.
- Prereferral intervention programs develop individualized plans designed to address the specific needs of each student, which keeps the interventions from being program driven.

Combined, the unique strengths of each program enhance the overall intervention efforts of schools and districts. So how does a school administrator do this? The process begins with those responsible for managing and leading intervention programs making several important decisions.

IMPLEMENTATION DECISIONS

An administrator considering establishing what will be referred to as the *systematic administration model of interventions* must make a choice between two options. The first option is to concentrate on implementing the program as described in Chapters 2–5, followed by strengthening the program through the addition of RTI model elements. One scenario for doing this is dedicating the first year of implementation to establishing a high-quality prereferral intervention program and then, in the second year, adding the following RTI components: universal screening procedures, analysis of classroom performance patterns, and tiered research-based interventions.

This option is the appropriate choice if the current prereferral intervention program is either poorly structured or poorly implemented because it enables the team to develop a solid foundation. Without a foundation built on high levels of group cohesiveness and strong collaborative problem-solving skills, prereferral intervention teams will not succeed.

The second option is to incorporate additional features into a "revised" prereferral intervention program from the very beginning. In this scenario, the administrator responsible for implementing the intervention program includes the additional features at the same time as he or she completes each of the four phases described in Chapters 2–5. This choice makes sense if the prereferral intervention team already uses effective group processes to develop high-quality intervention plans. In other words, the foundation required for successful task completion is already firmly in place.

UNIVERSAL SCREENING DECISIONS

Regardless of the sequence employed for implementation, the school administrator must make several additional decisions prior to establishing the systematic administration model of interventions. The first decision deals with the subject areas for which universal screening procedures will be established. Most school districts begin with reading and possibly written language skills. Considering that most of the students identified as having learning disabilities require assistance in these areas, this is a logical starting point.

The tools used for conducting the majority of universal screenings are curriculum probes. These are usually short, easy-to-administer assessments that attempt to compare students' current performance levels at a given moment in time with the anticipated levels of achievement as determined by grade-level expectations. These probes normally focus on academics but may seek to determine social or behavioral functioning.

Once the subject areas serving as the focus for universal screening procedures have been determined, the next decision concerns who will develop these probes. In other words, will the curriculum probes be commercially developed or will they be developed by school district personnel? Commercially developed probes such as the Dynamic Indicators of Basic Early Literacy Skills already have nationally established norms. Furthermore, they are relatively easy to implement because most of the materials have already been developed. On the other hand, curriculum probes developed by local school district personnel will be more aligned with the district's curriculum expectations. Thus, they may be more valuable for instructional purposes. This decision ultimately depends on the resources available and the purpose for administering the curriculum probes.

The final decision related to universal screening procedures concerns how often curriculum probes will be administered and by whom. Typically, curriculum probes are administered three to four times per year. Choosing who should administer these curriculum probes depends on the level of training required for administration and scoring as well as the level of professional behavior exhibited by staff.

If the administration and scoring of the curriculum probes is complex, it makes sense to have them administered by individuals who have received the appropriate training. School leaders will also want to use someone other than the student's teacher to administer and score the probes if they believe that staff members cannot be trusted to complete the task with integrity.

INTERVENTION TIER DECISIONS

Another set of leadership decisions relates to adding the intervention tiers. The first decision establishes how many tiers will exist. A defining characteristic of RTI models is the establishment of multiple intervention tiers, each of which is associated with the provision of different types of programs. Furthermore, as one moves up the tiers, the intensity level of the services increases.

Much like traditional prereferral intervention programs, the first tier typically provides high-quality instruction and/or behavioral supports within the general education environment. In Tier 1, it is common for the regular classroom teacher to make curricular and instructional modifications for the struggling student.

The second tier provides more specialized instruction for students whose performance and rate of progress significantly lags behind their peers. Tier 2 may include several subtiers and/or different types of interventions.

The final tier is designed to provide a comprehensive evaluation by a multidisciplinary team. The purpose of this Tier 3 evaluation is to determine whether the student has a disability and is therefore eligible for special education and related services.

Once the number of tiers has been established, decisions must be made about the nature of each tier. At a minimum, those responsible for planning this aspect of the systematic administration model of interventions must answer these three questions:

- How should the intervention management team decide on student placement into intervention tiers?
- Will there be rules for the minimum and/or maximum amount of time that a student remains in an intervention tier?
- What research-based intervention programs will be utilized in each tier, and who will deliver them?

The answer to the first question has two options. The first option for student placement into tiers is sequential, and if this is selected, then students must begin receiving interventions in Tier 1. If the interventions delivered in Tier 1 prove insufficient, then a student will progress to Tier 2. If the Tier 2 interventions prove insufficient, then a student is referred for a special education evaluation. The advantage of this model is that student placement and movement within tiers requires minimal decision making.

A second option is to place students into tiers based on identified student need, and if this is selected, then the intervention management team must use the data collected to determine the intensity of intervention required. For example, a student may be so significantly behind his or her peers in phonological awareness that the team decides to skip Tier 1 and move the student directly into a Tier 2 intervention. The advantage of this approach is that identified student needs determine the intensity level of interventions provided. However, this option requires team members to have a clear understanding of the purpose and programs used in each tier.

With regard to the question of minimum and maximum amounts of time in an intervention tier, without a doubt a minimum amount of time is necessary for most interventions to have the desired effect. Yet if an intervention is not showing the desired results after an extended period of time, then changes must be made. Some RTI models establish minimum and maximum times before a student may be moved from one tier to the next. An applied example of this rule is the requirement that a student must receive two marking periods of Tier 2 interventions prior to being referred for a special education evaluation. Although this approach ensures time for implementation of interventions, it does not take into account the individual nature of student needs.

Using the previously described approach for determining the effectiveness of interventions is the superior choice. In this case, the intervention management team decides on the desired outcome, the time frame for reaching this outcome, the means for assessing progress, and the rules to be applied for determining the need to change the intensity level of the interventions. This individualized approach to student movement between tiers encourages timely changes based on individual students response to the interventions implemented.

Answering the question about research-based programs and the responsibilities for delivering them depends greatly on the resources available in the school or district. A school or district with abundant resources will have many more choices than one with limited resources.

Although there are many possible configurations, for the sake of clarity consider the following real-world example. In a small K–8 school district with moderate resources, three tiers of intervention have been established for reading. The first involves instruction by the general education teacher using the Harcourt Trophies reading series. As part of an intervention plan, the general education teacher may modify her instructional practices or supplement the core program with supplemental components.

The second tier has two subtiers, each of which is delivered by a different teacher. Tier 2A is delivered by a basic skills teacher. The intervention management team and the basic skills teacher collaborate to develop groups of four to six students with common instructional needs (e.g., five fourth graders demonstrating moderate difficulties with oral reading fluency). The basic skills teacher delivers instruction to these students three times a week for 30 minutes using the Read Naturally program. This instruction supplements, rather than replaces, the regular classroom reading instruction.

Tier 2B is delivered by the district's reading specialist. In this case, the intervention management team has determined that a student requires intensive assistance. For example, a second grader is demonstrating severe difficulties with phonemic awareness and phonological tasks. For 30 minutes daily, the reading specialist works with the student one on one, using selected parts of the Wilson Language Fundations program to deliver instruction. Once again, the student continues to receive modified regular classroom instruction in the core reading program.

The third tier is special education. Students who are found to be eligible for special education and related services receive an individualized education plan (IEP). Using the goals and objectives of the IEP, a special education teacher delivers reading instruction in place of the regular classroom instruction, using a variety of research-based instructional materials matched to the student's needs to deliver instruction.

INTERVENTION MANAGEMENT TEAM TRAINING AND STAFF AWARENESS

To be effective, the intervention management team members will need further training. In addition to the training described in Chapter 4, they will need to learn how to interpret the results of the curriculum probes. Then they will need to learn how to use the probe results and teacher recommendations to determine the pool of at-risk students. Once they identify those students, the team members must be instructed in the method to be used for determining whether a classroom-level intervention should be considered. Last, the members of the team must have a clear understanding of the characteristics of each tier.

All staff members will need to learn about certain additional aspects of this intervention process, including the reason for administering the curriculum probes and the teachers' roles and responsibilities in the administration and scoring of these probes. If teachers are administering and scoring the probes, then they must be trained in the correct procedures for accomplishing this task. Additionally, all staff members must understand how movement between tiers occurs and the characteristics of each intervention tier.

THE COMBINED PROCESS

Figure 7.1 illustrates the steps of the systematic administration model of interventions. It is important to note that many of these

Figure 7.1   Systematic Administration Model of Interventions (also found in Resource B #22)

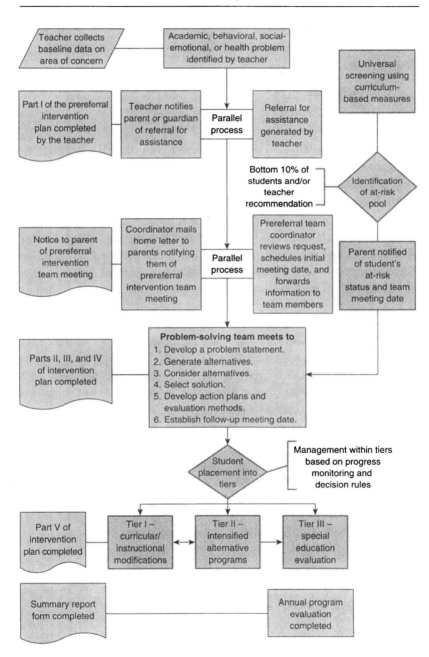

steps are the same as those in the prereferral intervention process (Figure 4.3). In Figure 7.1, these common steps are represented by the lighter-colored boxes. The differences begin with the universal screening on the far right-hand side, and the remainder of the darker boxes represents the features added to create the systematic administration model.

IDENTIFYING THE AT-RISK POOL

In addition to teacher referral, through this model students can become the focus of collaborative problem solving via the universal screening process. At predetermined points in the school year, the intervention management team will meet to examine the data collected during the universal screening process.

In analyzing the data, the team will look for two things. First, it will identify the students in the bottom 10th percentile. These are the students who are potentially at the highest level of risk. These students will need to be examined further to determine the need for additional intervention planning. This could be done by having the students' teacher(s) complete a teacher screening questionnaire to make sure that the assessment data collected during the universal screening process is an accurate measure of the students' typical classroom performance (see Figure 7.2). Likewise, students with scores above the 10th percentile may be entered into the at-risk pool by receiving a teacher recommendation.

Second, as part of the process the team must determine whether any class has a disproportionate number of students falling within the bottom 10th percentile. If so, it is possible that an administrator will need to facilitate a classroom-level intervention instead of one aimed at specific students. If a significant number of students in a heterogeneously grouped classroom perform at or below the median level of their school- or districtwide peers, it is probable that the problem does not reside within the students.

TIER PLACEMENT

Having identified the students who are not making adequate progress toward essential curricular objectives, the intervention management team will notify the parents of their student's

Figure 7.2   Sample Teacher Referral Form (also found in Resource B #23)

Teacher's name: Rhonda Williams

First Marking Period Results for Oral Reading Probes

Directions: Please review the information provided below to determine whether the score obtained by the student on the recently administered oral reading probes is an accurate assessment of his or her typical classroom performance. If you check "no" for any student, please attach a brief explanation with evidence describing why this performance was atypical.

Student's name	Score and percentile rank	Typical of classroom performance?
Jason Smith	12 out of 30 – 8th percentile	___ Yes ___ No
Denise Adams	11 out of 30 – 7th percentile	___ Yes ___ No
John Jamison	13 out of 30 – 9th percentile	___ Yes ___ No
Dana Sherman	8 out of 30 – 5th percentile	___ Yes ___ No

Please provide the names of students not on this list who should be considered by the prereferral intervention team for additional supports and services in this curricular area.

Student's name   Reason for concern

_____   _____

_____   _____

---

at-risk status and invite them to attend an intervention planning meeting. In this meeting, the team will use the established problem-solving approach to determine which intervention(s) to apply. However, unlike traditional prereferral intervention programs, in this model the team will choose from several tiers when selecting interventions. Just like in the prereferral intervention process, a student's intervention plan will include a specific time frame for implementing the intervention(s). Each intervention will be anchored to decision rules (generic decision rules are provided at the end of Chapter 4).

As assessment data continues to be gathered at the specified intervals, the established decision rules will be applied to determine whether to move the student into a different tier. Monitoring student progress and making decisions using the rules established will remain an ongoing focus for the meetings of the intervention management team.

If the interventions designed and coordinated by the team as part of Tiers 1 and 2 are implemented with fidelity but are not successful, it is unlikely that this is due to inadequacies in curriculum and instruction. At this point, multiple research-based approaches at different levels of intensity will have been attempted. Thus, it is now appropriate to look for the learning disability that may exist within the child.

If the decision is made to recommend an evaluation for eligibility for special education, then the parent must be asked for consent to conduct this evaluation. At this point, the coordinator of the intervention management team will complete a referral for special education evaluation. The referral will include an organized folder documenting the interventions attempted and the results received from each intervention. This information will be used by the IEP team to determine whether an assessment is warranted and, if so, which assessments should be done. If the student is eligible for special education and related services, the information may be used to develop the goals, objectives, and strategies to be addressed in the IEP.

CONCLUSION

Due to the similarities between prereferral intervention programs and RTI models, it makes sense to combine these two into one process. The systematic administration model of interventions described in this chapter combines these two programs by incorporating the unique strengths found in each. Implementing this model requires that educational leaders make additional decisions and provide further staff training. These decisions and training build on the prereferral intervention process described in Chapters 2–5. Although the effort and resources required to make these additions cannot be taken for granted, ultimately they will improve the coordination and effectiveness of the intervention services provided in a school district.

FINAL THOUGHTS

When staff members actively use intervention programs to develop strategies designed to meet the needs of challenging students, the school's professional learning community is enhanced. As educators see these programs as collaborative forums for problem solving, they will begin to view them as important.

This change will not be easy, though. Even when something does not work effectively, it is often valued because it is predictable. Paradoxically, some of the same staff members who express frustration with prereferral intervention teams will resist your attempts at changing them.

However, persisting in creating and managing intervention programs as they are described in this book will change them from bureaucratic necessities to powerful and productive structures. It will be then that you will have succeeded in moving beyond bureaucracy to capture the spirit of intervention programs. This shift from compliance to commitment will ensure a brighter future for your struggling students and their teachers.

Resource A

Putting It All Together: The Implementation Plan

There is a significant discrepancy between how prereferral intervention teams are described in research literature and how they are implemented in schools. What is so troubling about this disconnect is that prereferral intervention teams are supposed to be designed to assist teachers with the most challenging and perhaps neediest students. Those who need the services the most are on the receiving end of an inconsistently and often poorly applied model for providing services.

At least in part, this is due to educational leaders' lack of knowledge and skill in designing, managing, and leading these teams. Regardless of the reason for the current situation, there is good news. With systematic planning and focused effort, it is possible to rectify this situation.

At first, the actions described in this book may seem awkward. Until the process is firmly established, it may be necessary for the educational leader to have a checklist to follow. The following plan is a systematic strategy that can be used by any educational leader to bridge the gap between the status quo and the vision for effective prereferral intervention teams. Of course, this plan may have to be modified to take into account local issues or concerns.

PREREFERRAL INTERVENTION IMPLEMENTATION PLAN

Before the start of the school year

- Analyze and make decisions regarding the following:
  1. the costs and benefits of initiating or revising your school's prereferral intervention team
  2. the task to be achieved by the prereferral intervention team and the subsequent requirements for completing this task
  3. the level of authority that the prereferral intervention team will have over decisions and actions

- Plan and prepare to do the following:
  1. compose the team with the appropriate staff members
  2. communicate the task so that it is clear and motivating to prereferral intervention team members
  3. provide the educational, informational, and material resources that the team will need

- Complete and be prepared to share the Prereferral Intervention Team Charter.

During the first month of school

- Arrange for and conduct your team start-up meeting and your initial team training session.
- After having completed your initial team training session, provide a clear explanation to the rest of the faculty regarding the purpose of the prereferral intervention team, the responsibilities of the referring teacher, and the process that the team will use.
- Begin the yearlong process of providing process assistance as necessary and appropriate.

At the end of each marking period or trimester

- Facilitate a group reflection session. Combine this with a discussion focused on identifying and eliminating or minimizing barriers to successful task completion. Take action as necessary.

Near the middle and end of the school year

- Conduct an evaluation of the team's activities by compiling and analyzing the data provided by the three tools described in Chapter 6. Using the Priority-Setting Matrix (Figure 6.7) as a guide, complete the Strategic Action Planning Form (Figure 6.8).

At the end of the school year

- Facilitate a group celebration to recognize the efforts of the prereferral intervention team members.
- For those leaders seeking to implement the systematic administration model of interventions described in Chapter 7, the following steps will be added either as part of the Year 1 plan or as an extension in Year 2.

Before the start of the next school year

- Analyze and make decisions regarding the following:
  1. what subject areas will be the focus of universal screening procedures
  2. whether the curriculum probes used will be commercially or district-developed
  3. who will administer and score the probes and how often this will be done
  4. how many intervention tiers will exist
  5. how placement into the tiers will be managed
  6. which research-based programs will be used in each tier and who will deliver them

During the first month of school

- Train the intervention management team in the interpretation of universal screening measures.
- Make sure that the intervention management team understands the nature of each tier as well as progression between tiers.
- Familiarize the intervention management team with the research-based intervention programs available in the school district.

- Inform all staff members of the changes related to the intervention program. Pay special attention to explaining the administration and use of the universal screening measures as well as the nature of each intervention tier.

At predetermined points during the school year

- Administer and score the universal screening measures.
- Gather the team to identify which students are in the bottom 10th percentile.
- Examine patterns between classrooms. If necessary, implement classroom-level interventions.
- Identify students who require intervention plans.
- Conduct collaborative problem-solving activities that lead to intervention plans.
- Place students in tiers based on intervention plans.

Ongoing

- Meet to analyze ongoing assessment data. Make decisions about student movement between tiers based on the decision rules established in the intervention plans.

Resource B

Implementation Tools

RESOURCE B #1
Prereferral Intervention Team Charter

Core Team Members	

Team's Task

Effectiveness Criteria

Task Parameters	
Must always do	Must never do

Educational Resources		
Name	Knowledge and skill	How to access

Information Resources	
Type of data	Location

Material Resources (clerical support, space, time, supplies, and materials)

RESOURCE B #2

Task Redefinition Activity

Purpose

To achieve common understanding about the task to be completed.

Basics

Number of participants: 4–12

Time needed: 20 – 40 minutes, depending on group size

Materials: pens or pencils, chart paper, and markers

Procedures

1. The educational leader presents the committee with the task to be completed by reading it aloud and providing it in writing.
2. The educational leader removes the written description of the task and provides committee members with time to write down their thoughts to complete this statement: "The task for the school's prereferral intervention team is . . ."
3. Each committee member pairs with a partner, and they share their responses. The partners write down the ideas that they have in common or agree on.
4. Sets of partners combine to make foursomes, and the process is repeated.
5. The groups' responses are shared with the educational leader. The leader notes and discusses with the group any discrepancies that arise. Whole-group discussion should occur as required.
6. If necessary, the task description is rewritten so that all parties can reach agreement about what the task is and what it requires.

RESOURCE B #3

Team Norms Activity

Purpose

To establish norms that will be conducive to group functioning.

Basics

Number of participants: at least four

Time needed: 20–40 minutes

Materials: chart paper and markers

Directions

1. Using a team as an example, the leader introduces the idea of staff meeting agreements.

   - We have all been part of teams. In any team there are certain rules or expectations for what we could or couldn't do and how we would behave. What were some of the rules or expectations on teams you have been a part of? (Facilitate sharing of responses.)
   - Most of what has been suggested are rules that helped the team work successfully as a group. Just like these teams, ours must have agreements or expectations to help the group function effectively. What are some of the behaviors, both positive and negative, that you have experienced as a member of a team? (Record the responses on a T-Chart.)

   Example:

<u>Positive Team Behaviors</u>	<u>Negative Team Behaviors</u>
Be on time.	Engage in side conversation.
Come prepared.	Dominate the discussion.
Focus on the task.	Do other work.

(Continued)

(Continued)

2. Initiate a group discussion about the messages that the behaviors listed in each column send to team members.

3. Lead the group in a discussion about the value of having a set of basic agreements for committee meetings. After reviewing a sample of possible agreements, have members add other possible agreements to the list. Continue adding these until the members believe that they have exhausted the possibilities.

   Sample Agreements

   * We will start and end meetings on time.
   * We will actively listen to each other's ideas and opinions.
   * We will make important decisions through consensus.
   * We will remain focused on the topic or task.

4. Have team members divide a piece of paper into three equal columns. Next, inform staff members that they have 100 points that they may "spend" among each of the sample agreements listed. As points are spent on one agreement, they are subtracted from the total of 100. Points represent the importance that the team members place on a particular agreement.

5. After completing the task individually, team members should share there scores in groups of three to four. The discussions that often follow this activity help clarify team members' thinking about the agreements. They often share more poignant examples to illustrate why they value a particular outcome over another.

6. After this small-group sharing, the personal points are distributed again. The educational leader then collects all of the sheets and tallies how many points were spent on each item. Only the second score should be counted toward the group's final agreements.

RESOURCE B #4

Overhead Transparency: Prereferral Intervention Process

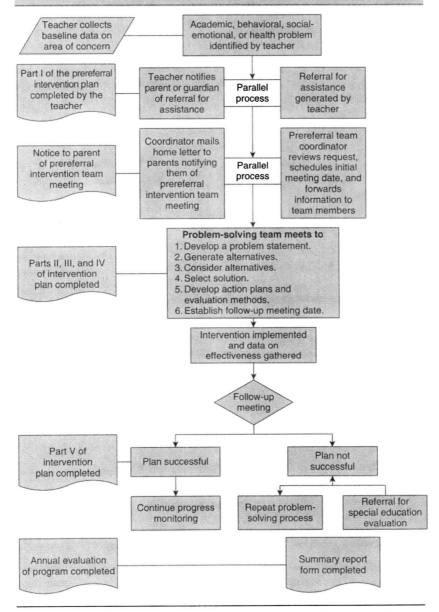

Teacher collects baseline data on area of concern

Academic, behavioral, social-emotional, or health problem identified by teacher

Part I of the prereferral intervention plan completed by the teacher

Teacher notifies parent or guardian of referral for assistance

Parallel process

Referral for assistance generated by teacher

Notice to parent of prereferral intervention team meeting

Coordinator mails home letter to parents notifying them of prereferral intervention team meeting

Parallel process

Prereferral team coordinator reviews request, schedules initial meeting date, and forwards information to team members

Parts II, III, and IV of intervention plan completed

Problem-solving team meets to
1. Develop a problem statement.
2. Generate alternatives.
3. Consider alternatives.
4. Select solution.
5. Develop action plans and evaluation methods.
6. Establish follow-up meeting date.

Intervention implemented and data on effectiveness gathered

Follow-up meeting

Part V of intervention plan completed

Plan successful

Plan not successful

Continue progress monitoring

Repeat problem-solving process

Referral for special education evaluation

Annual evaluation of program completed

Summary report form completed

RESOURCE B #5

Prereferral Intervention Plan

I. Referral Documentation

Student's name: _____ Grade: _____ Teacher: _____
Student's address: _____ Phone number: _____
Gender: ___ Ethnicity: ___ English language proficiency: _____
Free or reduced lunch ☐
Referral date: _____
Parent has been notified of this referral ☐
Primary reason for referral (check only one)
☐   Academic concern   ☐   Behavior concern
☐   Social concern   ☐   Health concern
☐   Other

II. Referral (All statements must be in observable, measurable terms)

Student performance desired in the classroom: _____
Current student performance (baseline data): _____

Interventions attempted	Results

Other relevant information the team should consider: _____

III. Problem Analysis

Date and time of initial problem-solving meeting: _____
Meeting participants: _____
Problem statement: _____
Generation of alternatives:

Option	Advantages	Disadvantages

Teacher-selected alternative(s): _____

IV. Intervention Plan

Objective: By _____, _____ will demonstrate the ability to _____, as measured by _____.

Strategies to be implemented:

Strategy	Person responsible	When

Consultant: _____
Method(s) for collecting data and monitoring progress: _____
Date and time of initial follow-up meeting: _____

V. Plan Review

Date and time of meeting: _____
Meeting participants: _____

Identified concern	Baseline performance	Post-intervention

Next Steps

- ☐ Plan successful; continue monitoring progress.
- ☐ Plan not successful; repeat problem-solving process.
- ☐ Plan not successful; refer for special education evaluation.

RESOURCE B #6
Overhead Transparency: Step 1

Step 1: Problem Identification

- Teacher

  o defines problem

  o requests assistance

  o notifies parent

  o submits referral form

- Team Coordinator

  o reviews form

  o schedules initial team meeting

  o notifies team members

Step 2: Problem Analysis

- Resource Group

    o validates problem statement

    o identifies variables contributing to the problem

    o generates ideas and solutions

- Referring Teacher

    o chooses strategy to implement

- Team Coordinator

    o facilitates completion of documentation

    o facilitates identification of consultant

    o schedules initial follow-up meeting

RESOURCE B #8
Problem Statement Validation Questions (Handout 1)

- Can you give a specific example of what you mean by _____?

- In your class, what would we actually see that would mean _____ to you?

- What specific task is this student having difficulty completing?

- What response is expected of the student that he or she is not providing currently?

- Is the concern one of the quantity produced or of the quality of the product?

- If we were in your class observing this student, what would we see in relation to the problem you have identified?

- Do you see this problem primarily resulting from a lack of skill, knowledge, motivation, or something else?

- How does this student's problem compare with the functioning of other students in your class?

RESOURCE B #9

Problem Analysis Questions (Handout 2)

Behavioral

- In what other settings or classes does this behavior occur?
- If it doesn't occur in other settings, what accounts for the difference?
- What happens just before the behavior occurs?
- What happens just after the behavior occurs?

Academic

- How do you give directions for completing the task?
- How does the student receive the information (e.g., orally, visually)?
- How is the student expected to respond (e.g., writing, reading, spoken)?
- How much practice is provided for completing this type of task?
- What kind of feedback do you give the student? How often?
- How does the student perform when assisted?
- What type of assistance works?

General

- What does the student do well?
- What are times when things are better?
- What is different about those times when things are better?

RESOURCE B #10

Consultant's Role (Handout 3)

- The consultant is an individual trained in and experienced with implementing the recommended assessment and intervention strategies. He or she may or may not be a member of the preferral intervention team.

- The consultant's objective is to ensure that the referring teacher has the knowledge and skills necessary for implementing the agreed-upon intervention strategies.

- At a minimum, the consulting process shall include the following:

  o providing any relevant literature to the referring teacher to read prior to conducting the in-class demonstration

  o conducting an in-class demonstration for the referring teacher to observe

  o observing and coaching the referring teacher in the implementation of the process

  o providing ongoing opportunities for the referring teacher to ask questions and seek feedback on implementation efforts

RESOURCE B #11

Overhead Transparency: Step 3

Step 3: Plan Implementation

- Referring teacher

  o implements plan

  o monitors implementation results

  o seeks assistance from team coordinator and consultant as necessary

- Team Coordinator

  o meets with referring teacher and, when appropriate, the consultant

  o serves as link to resource team

RESOURCE B #12

Overhead Transparency: Step 4

Step 4: Plan Review

- Teacher and Prereferral Intervention Team

  - ○ compare student's pre- and postintervention performance

  - ○ decide on next steps

RESOURCE B #13

Prereferral Intervention Team Reflection Form

Directions: For each of the items below, please circle the response that indicates your level of agreement with the statement.

1 = strongly disagree   2 = disagree   3 = agree   4 = strongly agree

1.	We start our meetings on time.	1	2	3	4
2.	We end our meetings on time.	1	2	3	4
3.	We actively listen to each other's ideas and opinions.	1	2	3	4
4.	We weight the opinions of team members based on their knowledge and skill.	1	2	3	4
5.	During meetings we remain focused on the topic or task.	1	2	3	4
6.	We come to meetings having done the necessary preparations for completing the task.	1	2	3	4

Please Write a Brief Comment for Each of the Following Statements:

One thing that our team is doing well, which we want to continue, is:

One thing that our team could do better to function more effectively and efficiently would be:

Collective Goal Statement (to be completed by team)

Our collective goal is:

To achieve this goal we will:

We know that we will have achieved this goal when:

RESOURCE B #14
Prereferral Intervention Team Report

School: _____ Data organized by: _____
Date completed: _____

I. Total Number of Referrals: _____

II. Referrals by Grade Level

Grade level	Number of referrals	Percentage of total
K		
1		
2		
3		
4		
5		
6		
7		
8		
9		
10		
11		
12		

III. Referrals by Ethnicity

Ethnicity	Number of referrals	Percentage of total
White		
Black		
Hispanic/Latino		
Asian/Pacific Islander		
American Indian/Alaskan		

IV. Referrals by English Language Proficiency

Language proficiency	Number of referrals	Percentage of total
English only		
Limited English proficient		
Fluent English		

V. Referrals by Free or Reduced Lunch

Free or reduced lunch	Number of referrals	Percentage of total
Eligible		
Not eligible		

VI. Primary Reason for Referral

Characteristic	Academic		Behavior		Social		Health		Other	
	No.	%	No.	%	No.	%	No.	%	No.	%
K										
1										
2										
3										
4										
5										
6										
7										
8										
9										
10										
11										
12										
White										
Black										
Hispanic/Latino										
Asian/Pacific Islander										
American Indian/Alaskan										
English only										
Limited English proficient										
Fluent English										
Free or reduced lunch										

(Continued)

(Continued)

VII. Outcome of Referrals

Characteristic	Initial plan successful		Revised plan successful		Referral for evaluation	
	No.	%	No.	%	No.	%
K						
1						
2						
3						
4						
5						
6						
7						
8						
9						
10						
11						
12						
White						
Black						
Hispanic/Latino						
Asian/Pacific Islander						
American Indian/ Alaskan						
English only						
Limited English proficient						
Fluent English						
Free or reduced lunch						

RESOURCE B #15

Prereferral Intervention Team Rating Scale

Thank you for taking the time to complete this survey on our school's prereferral intervention team. Please answer *all* of the following statements by circling *one* of the five responses provided in the columns.

(A) Always   (M) Most of the time   (S) Some of the time   (R) Rarely   (N) Never

1. The tasks to be achieved by the team were clear.   A M S R N

2. The tasks to be achieved by the team were motivating.   A M S R N

3. The team had the level of authority necessary for effectively completing the assigned tasks.   A M S R N

4. The composition of the team helped with the completion of the tasks. A M S R N

5. The team had access to the information necessary for completing the tasks.   A M S R N

6. The team had access to the outside expertise necessary for completing the tasks.   A M S R N

7. Team members felt rewarded for completing the assigned tasks.   A M S R N

(Continued)

(Continued)

---

8. The team had the necessary material resources for completing the assigned tasks. A M S R N

9. It was clearly understood who was a member of this team. A M S R N

10. The norms and roles used by the team were helpful for completing the assigned tasks. A M S R N

11. As a team, we had an opportunity to discuss with the school leadership any barriers that were impeding the group's performance. A M S R N

12. As a team, we received assistance that helped us improve our group process. A M S R N

13. As a team, we stopped periodically to reflect on and learn from our experiences. A M S R N

14. I found the experience of serving on this team personally satisfying. A M S R N

15. The experience of being on this team increased my skills in working as a member of a group. A M S R N

RESOURCE B #16

Prereferral Intervention Team Rating Scale Tabulation Worksheet

Question #	(A) – 4	(M) – 3	(S) – 2	(R) – 1	(N) – 0	Average
1						
2						
3						
4						
5						
6						
7						
8						
9						
10						
11						
12						
13						
14						
15						
	_____	/15 =	_____			
	Group		Group			
	Total		Rating			

RESOURCE B #17

Teacher Satisfaction Survey

Recently you participated in a prereferral intervention team plan review meeting. This survey is designed to determine your level of satisfaction with the overall prereferral intervention process. Please answer *all* of the following statements by circling *one* of the five responses provided in the columns.

(SA) Strongly Agree   (A) Agree   (N) Neutral   (D) Disagree   (SD) Strongly Disagree

1. The amount of time required for completing the prereferral intervention process was reasonable.   SA A N D SD

2. The paperwork required for completing the prereferral intervention process was reasonable.   SA A N D SD

3. The intervention strategies developed as a result of the prereferral intervention process were things I did not think of on my own.   SA A N D SD

4. The intervention strategies developed as a result of the prereferral intervention process could be realistically implemented in my classroom.   SA A N D SD

5. I received the material resources needed for implementing the intervention strategies developed.   SA A N D SD

6. I received the emotional support   SA A N D SD
   required for implementing the
   intervention strategies developed.

7. I received training in the knowledge   SA A N D SD
   and skills necessary for implementing
   the interventions.

8. If confronted with a similar student   SA A N D SD
   concern in the future, I will feel more
   confident in my ability to
   independently solve the problem.

9. As a result of the prereferral   SA A N D SD
   intervention team experience, I have
   improved my skills for working with
   students who experience academic or
   behavioral problems.

10. I would recommend using the services   SA A N D SD
    of the prereferral intervention team
    to my colleagues.

Suggestions I have for improving the prereferral intervention process include:

RESOURCE B #18
Teacher Satisfaction Survey Tabulation Worksheet

Question #	(SA) – 5	(A) – 4	(N) – 3	(D) – 2	(SD) – 1	Average
1						
2						
3						
4						
5						
6						
7						
8						
9						
10						
	_____	/10 =	_____			
	Group		Group			
	Total		Rating			

RESOURCE B #19

Prereferral Intervention Team Observation Form

Date: _____

Observer: _____

	Observed	Not Observed
Baseline data for the student's area of concern was described in specific, measurable terms.		
The desired student replacement behavior was described in specific, observable terms.		
The team validated the accuracy of the teacher-provided problem statement.		
The team identified variables that potentially contributed to the student's behavior.		
The team brainstormed potential interventions to address the concern presented.		

(Continued)

(Continued)

	Observed	Not Observed
The team identified potential advantages and disadvantages for each of the options brainstormed.		
The teacher selected an option(s) to implement as an intervention for addressing the student concern.		
The option(s) selected by the teacher has been translated into a specific, measurable goal statement.		
Responsibilities for carrying out the tasks for implementing the intervention(s) have been clearly identified.		
Methods and responsibilities for monitoring student progress have been clearly identified.		

Positive behaviors observed:

Recommendations/suggestions:

RESOURCE B #20

Priority-Setting Matrix

Area of Concern	Impact Rate each item 1–5, with 5 having the greatest impact.	Effort Rate each item 1–5, with 5 requiring the least amount of effort.	Feasibility Rate each item 1–5, with 5 being the most feasible.	Total of Individual Ratings	Individual Ranking Rank order three items only, with 5 as highest priority, 3 as second highest, and 1 as lowest.	Group Ranking

RESOURCE B #21

Strategic Action Planning Form

Area in need of improvement	Action steps	Individual(s) responsible	Timeline	Evaluation

RESOURCE B #22

Systematic Administration Model of Interventions

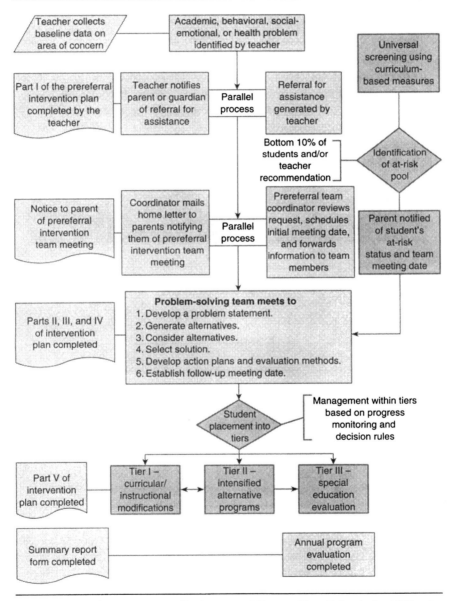

RESOURCE B #23
Teacher Referral Form

Teacher's name:

Date:

Assessment results for:

Directions: Please review the information provided below to determine whether the score obtained by the student on the recently administered probes is an accurate assessment of his or her typical classroom performance. If you check "no" for any student, please attach a brief explanation with evidence describing why this performance was atypical.

Student's name	Score and percentile rank	Typical of classroom performance?
		___ Yes ___ No
		___ Yes ___ No
		___ Yes ___ No
		___ Yes ___ No
		___ Yes ___ No

Please provide the names of students not on this list who should be considered by the prereferral intervention team for additional supports and services in this curricular area.

Student's name   Reason for concern

_____   _____

_____   _____

_____   _____

References

Askamit, D. L., & Rankin, J. L. (1993). Problem-solving teams as a prereferral process. *Special Services in the Schools, 7*(1), 1–25.

Bahr, M. W., & Kovaleski, J. F. (2006). The need for problem-solving teams. *Remedial and Special Education, 27*, 2–5.

Bahr, M. W., Whitten, E., Dieker, L., Kocarek, C. E., & Manson, D. (1999). A comparison of school-based intervention teams: Implications for educational and legal reform. *Exceptional Children, 66*, 67–84.

Buck, G. H., Polloway, E. A., Smith-Thomas, A., & Cook, K. W. (2003). Prereferral intervention processes: A survey of state practices. *Exceptional Children, 69*, 349–360.

Flugum, K. R., & Reschly, D. J. (1994). Prereferral interventions: Quality indices and outcomes. *Journal of School Psychology, 32*, 1–14.

Fuchs, D., Fuchs, L., Bahr, M. W., Fernstrom, P., & Stecker, P. M. (1990). Prereferral intervention: A prescriptive approach. *Exceptional Children, 56*, 493–513.

Hackman, J. R. (2002). *Leading teams: Setting the stage for great performances.* Boston: Harvard University Press.

Kovaleski, J. F. (2002). Best practices in operating pre-referral intervention teams. In A. Thomas & J. Grimes (Eds.), *Best practices in school psychology IV* (pp. 645–656). Washington DC: National Association of School Psychologists.

Kovaleski, J. F., & Glew, M. C. (2006). Bringing instructional support teams to scale: Implications of the Pennsylvania experience. *Remedial and Special Education, 27*, 16–25.

Kruger, L. J., Struzziero, J., Watts, R., & Vacca, D. (1995). The relationship between organizational support and satisfaction with teacher assistance teams. *Remedial and Special Education, 16*, 203–211.

Moreland, R. L., Argote, L., & Krishnan, R. (1998). Training people to work in groups. In R. S. Tindale, L. Heath, J. Edwards, E. J. Posavac, F. B. Bryant, J. Myers, et al. (Eds.), *Theory and research on small groups* (pp. 37–60). New York: Plenum Press.

O'Shaugnessy, T. E., Lane, K. L., Gresham, F. M., & Beebe-Frankenberger, M. E. (2003). Children placed at risk for learning and behavioral difficulties: Implementing a school-wide system of early identification and intervention. *Remedial and Special Education, 24,* 27–35.

Rafoth, M. A., & Foriska, T. (2006). Administrator participation in promoting effective problem-solving teams. *Remedial and Special Education, 27,* 130–135.

Safran, S. P., & Safran, J. S. (1996). Intervention assistance programs and prereferral intervention teams: Directions for the twenty-first century. *Remedial and Special Education, 17,* 363–369.

Sindelar, P. T., Griffin, C. G., Smith, S. W., & Watanabe, A. K. (1992). Prereferral intervention: Encouraging notes on preliminary findings. *Elementary School Journal, 92,* 245–258.

Truscott, S. D., Cohen, C. E., Sams, D. P., Sanborn, K. J., & Frank, A. J. (2005). The current state(s) of prereferral intervention teams: A report from two national surveys. *Remedial and Special Education, 26,* 130–140.

Index

LaVergne, TN USA
25 March 2010
177122LV00004B/38/P

9 781412 966917